BOUNDARIES
WITH TEENS

Resources by Henry Cloud and John Townsend

Boundaries

Boundaries Workbook

Boundaries audio

Boundaries video curriculum

Boundaries in Dating

Boundaries in Dating Workbook

Boundaries in Dating audio

Boundaries in Dating curriculum

Boundaries in Marriage

Boundaries in Marriage Workbook

Boundaries in Marriage audio

Boundaries in Marriage curriculum

Boundaries with Kids

Boundaries with Kids Workbook

Boundaries with Kids audio

Boundaries with Kids curriculum

Changes That Heal (Cloud)

Changes That Heal Workbook (Cloud)

Changes That Heal audio (Cloud)

Hiding from Love (Townsend)

How People Grow

How People Grow Workbook

How People Grow audio

How to Have That Difficult Conversation You've Been Avoiding

Making Small Groups Work

Making Small Groups Work audio

The Mom Factor

The Mom Factor Workbook

Raising Great Kids

Raising Great Kids audio

Raising Great Kids for Parents of Preschoolers curriculum

Raising Great Kids Workbook for Parents of Preschoolers

Raising Great Kids Workbook for Parents of School-Age Children

Raising Great Kids Workbook for Parents of Teenagers

Safe People

Safe People Workbook

12 "Christian" Beliefs That Can Drive You Crazy

BOUNDARIES
WITH TEENS

WHEN TO SAY **YES**, HOW TO SAY **NO**

DR. JOHN **TOWNSEND**

(COAUTHOR OF THE BESTSELLING *BOUNDARIES*)

ZONDERVAN™

GRAND RAPIDS, MICHIGAN 49530 USA

ZONDERVAN.COM/
AUTHORTRACKER

ZONDERVAN™

Boundaries with Teens
Copyright © 2006 by John Townsend

This title is also available as a Zondervan ebook product. Visit www.zondervan.com/ebooks for more information.

This title is also available as a Zondervan audio product. Visit www.zondervan.com/audiopages for more information.

Requests for information should be addressed to:

Zondervan, *Grand Rapids, Michigan 49530*

Library of Congress Cataloging-in-Publication Data
Townsend, John Sims, 1952–.
    Boundaries with teens : when to say yes, how to say no / John Townsend.—1st ed.
      p. cm.
    Includes bibliographical references.
    ISBN-13: 978-0-310-25957-2
    ISBN-10: 0-310-25957-6
    1. Parent and teenager—Religious aspects—Christianity. 2. Child rearing—
Religious aspects—Christianity. 3. Parenting—Religious aspects—Christianity.
4. Teenagers—Conduct of life. I. Title.
    BV4529.T685 2006
    649'.125—dc22

                                                 2005024426

This edition printed on acid-free paper.

Published in association with Yates & Yates, LLP, Attorneys and Counselors, Orange, CA.

Interior design by Melissa Elenbaas

Printed in the United States of America

06 07 08 09 10 11 • 22 21 20 19 18 17 16 15 14 13 12 11 10 9 8 7 6 5 4 3 2 1

*To all those who are engaged in helping teens
navigate safely into adulthood.
Your love and effort will not be in vain.
God bless you.*

The mistake that Sharon and I both made, and we both agree on this, is we never set any boundaries.

Ozzy Osbourne

Contents

PART FOUR
Address Common Problems

ACKNOWLEDGMENTS

To my wife, Barbi, for being such a supportive and loving partner, as together we parent our teens;

To Ricky and Benny Townsend, for being such great kids, especially during these adolescent years;

To Scott Bolinder, publisher at Zondervan, for his support for, and belief in, the importance of the subject;

To my editor Sandy Vander Zicht, for her vision for this book's creation and her love for the written word;

To my editor Liz Heaney, for her diligence and care in the process of making a book readable;

To my agent, Sealy Yates, and his associate, Jeana Ledbetter, for their steadfast wisdom and protection of the writing process;

To my friends who have parented teens and provided me with lots of helpful information and stories: Roger and Diane Braff, Jim Burns, Cindy Canale, Cathy Evangelatos, Belinda Falk, Eric and Debbie Heard, Mark Holt, Jim Liebelt, Tom and Martha McCall, Dr. Paul Meier, Dr. Jerry Reddix, Ted and Jen Trubenbach, Bob Whiton;

To my adolescent specialist friends who reviewed chapters and made helpful comments: Dr. John Barrett, Dr. Tom Okamoto, and Brett Veltman;

To Dr. Jim Pugh, for his wisdom and experience in the fields of adolescents and of families;

To the Junior High Ministry of Mariners Church in Irvine, California, especially Chris Lagerlof, Ryan Schulte, Michael Siebert, Sabrina Garcia, whose tenures with the junior high ministry at

Mariners Church have helped so many kids, including mine, to find God, growth, and healthy relationships;

To the junior high small groups guys: Nate Barrett, Josh Bennar, Monty Buchanan, Zak Fuentes, Josh Hervey, Renny Martinez, and Travis Waddell, for being great kids and followers of God;

To my friend and writing partner, Dr. Henry Cloud, for his diligence and depth of thought in dealing with parenting and growth issues;

And a special thanks to my assistant, Janet Williams, who glues my work universe together, day after day, with care and good humor.

Who Threw the Switch?

I had known Trevor since he was six, because our families ran in the same circles. As a preteen, he was a normal kid, not perfect, but not out of control either. He was respectful of adults and fun to be around.

Then, when he was thirteen or fourteen, my wife, Barbi, our kids, and I ran into him and his mom, Beth, at a movie theater one night, and we adults started talking. It wasn't long before all of the kids started getting restless, particularly Trevor. He and his mom had a conversation that went something like this:

"Mom, I wanna go."

"Just a minute, honey."

"I said I wanna go!"

Beth looked a little embarrassed and said, "Trevor, we're almost done talking, okay?"

"HEY! I—SAID—I—WANT—TO—GO!"

People standing around in the theater began looking over at our little group.

His mom looked mortified. His face was a little flushed, but he didn't look at all self-conscious. He had only one thing on his mind— getting his mom moving.

She quickly said her good-byes, and the two of them left.

This encounter sticks in my mind because of the huge contrast between the Trevor who used to be and the Trevor who now was. It was as if a switch had been thrown. Whatever respect he'd once had for his mom, and likely others, had been greatly diminished.

Perhaps you can relate to Beth's experience as a parent. You may have an adolescent who, as a preteen, was more compliant and easier to connect with. Or perhaps you saw seeds of trouble in your child's preteen years, only to watch those seeds sprout when adolescence hit. Or maybe your child doesn't seem that much different, just bigger and stronger. In any case, it all points to the reality that *parenting teens is not like parenting at any other age, because children change dramatically during their teenage years.*

The Challenges Parents of Teens Face

Parents face many different issues and struggles in their efforts to parent their teens effectively, as demonstrated in this list of typical adolescent behaviors:

- has a disrespectful attitude toward parents, family, and others
- challenges requests or rules
- is self-absorbed and unable to see things from anyone else's perspective
- is lazy and careless about responsibilities
- has a negative attitude toward life, school, or people
- is emotionally withdrawn and distant from you
- has a tendency to pick friends of whom you disapprove
- erupts in anger that sometimes seems to come out of nowhere
- lacks motivation for school and fails to maintain grades
- neglects home chores and responsibilities
- has mood shifts that seem to have neither rhyme nor reason
- is mean to siblings or friends
- lacks interest in spiritual matters
- detaches from family events and wants to be with friends only
- lies and is deceptive about activities
- is physically aggressive and violent

- is truant from school or runs away
- abuses substances — alcohol, drugs, pornography, and so on
- engages in sexual activity

This list could go on, of course. It's no wonder that when faced with one or several of these problems, many parents become discouraged, overwhelmed, or confused about what to do. You don't have to be one of them. If you are reading this book because your teen exhibits any of the above behaviors, be encouraged. These problems have solutions. You don't have to resign yourself to simply coping and surviving for the next few years. Life with your teen can be much better than that. You can take some steps that can make major differences in the troublesome attitudes and behavior of your adolescent.

I have seen many teens become more responsible, happier, and better prepared for adult life after their parents began to apply the principles and techniques discussed in this book. Many of these teens not only made positive changes in their lives, but they also reconnected with their parents at levels that the parents had thought they would never experience again. These principles work — if you work them.

Teens Need Boundaries

The problems listed earlier all have a common foundation: *the battle between the teen's desire for total freedom and the parents' desire for total control.* All teens want the freedom to do what they want when they want. They need to learn that freedom is earned and that they can gain freedom by demonstrating responsibility. Adolescence is the time in life when kids are supposed to learn this lesson.

By the same token, parents need to be able to recognize when they are being overcontrolling and when they are being healthy and appropriate about saying "no." They need to be able to make this distinction in order to do their job: helping teens learn responsibility and self-control so that they use freedom appropriately and live well in the real world. To do this, parents must help teens learn boundaries.

I cannot overstate the importance of your role here. In the midst of your teen's demands, tantrums, threats, and acting out, your task is to sift through the craziness and lovingly set firm, appropriate limits.

When your teen behaves responsibly, you can loosen the reins a little and grant more freedom. You are the clear voice of sanity in your child's world. Your teen needs your voice and your help in learning how to set boundaries.

What are boundaries? Simply put, boundaries are one's personal property line. They are how you define yourself, say who you are and who you are not, set limits, and establish consequences if people are attempting to control you. When you say "no" to someone's bad behavior, you are setting a boundary. Boundaries are good for you and good for the other person, for boundaries help people clarify what they are and are not responsible for in life. (For a fuller treatment of boundaries, please refer to the book Dr. Henry Cloud and I wrote: *Boundaries: When to Say Yes, When to Say No, to Take Control of Your Life*.)[1]

Because of all the developmental changes teens are going through, they often don't have good control over their behavior, a clear sense of responsibility for their actions, or much self-discipline and structure. Instead, they often show disrespect of authority (as in Trevor's case), impulsiveness, irresponsibility, misbehavior, and erratic behavior. They are, as the Bible describes it, "like a wave of the sea, blown and tossed by the wind."[2]

Teens need to develop good boundaries in order to make it successfully through this season of life. Healthy boundaries give them the structure, self-control, and sense of ownership they need to figure out all their "who am I?" questions and to deal with the physiological and developmental changes they are experiencing.

Boundaries function somewhat like the trunk of a tree. The trunk holds the leaves, fruit, and roots together. However, all trees with strong trunks started out as weak saplings. They needed to be tied to a stake because they couldn't yet handle their own weight. They needed to lean on and be supported by something outside themselves. Then, in time, the trees matured and took over that job for themselves.

The process of developing boundaries is similar. Teens can't create their own "trunks." They don't have the necessary tools to become responsible, thoughtful, and empathetic with others. Like a tree sapling, they need help from outside themselves. Parents are the stake for their teens. They are the temporary external structure teens need in their last launch into real life. When parents tell teens the truth, set limits, establish curfews, confront misbehavior, and do a host of other things, they are providing a structure and helping teens to develop a structure. If all goes well, teens will ultimately and safely discard their parents' structure and, using their own structure, be able to meet the demands of adult life and responsibility.

And that is the purpose of this book, to show you how to help your adolescent shoulder responsibility for her actions, attitudes, and speech so that she learns the gift of self-control and ownership over her life. The whole process starts with you, the parent. So in this book you will learn a deceptively simple skill that all parents of teens need: knowing *when to say Yes, and how to say No,* that is how to implement and enforce healthy, loving boundaries with your adolescent.

After reading this you may think, *I don't really have good boundaries either. How can I dispense what I don't possess?* That is a common and important concern. A teen without boundaries needs a parent with boundaries. You'll find help for how to do this in the first part of this book, which teaches and equips you to develop your own personal limits so that you can transmit what you know and who you are to your teen.

Get the Big Picture

What are your goals and desires for your teen? Do you want some peace and quiet around the house? Less disrespect? No involvement with alcohol or drugs? Better school performance? More consideration for the needs and feelings of others?

It is easy for parents of teens to lose perspective and a sense of what is really important. They get no help from teens, who live in the present; it's all about what they are doing this second. Teenagers have little interest in, awareness of, or concern about the future. They live their lives pushing the *Urgent* button. That's why parents need to create an *Important* button for themselves and their teen. They need to guide their children in the right direction.

You will probably have to work a bit on this double perspective, because it doesn't come naturally. I can remember when one of my kids and I were discussing how late he should be able to go out with his friends one night. My son said, "You don't see it the right way."

I had no problem with his words, but I found his tone disrespectful and sarcastic. So I said, "That sounds disrespectful."

"I don't think I was disrespectful," he responded.

We went round and round about that, and I found myself getting focused on winning this battle. It became for me less about whether he had been disrespectful and more about winning the argument (not a helpful goal with teens, by the way). But at some point, I noticed both of us getting angrier and more entrenched in our positions. I thought to myself, *You're forgetting the big picture—the "future" orientation. How is this interaction with my son helping to prepare him for adulthood?* So I said, "Okay. We see your attitude differently. I'd like your tone to be warmer and less sarcastic and to sound more like this," at which point I used the tone I thought was respectful. Then I said, "What I heard was this," and I used the tone I had heard from him. "So from now on, that's how I'd like to be talked to when we disagree." My son agreed to that. And to this point, he has tried to keep a civil tone with me and other adults.

I wanted my son to see that in the adult world, it is important to clarify matters before you make a decision, just to make sure that everyone involved is aware of what is expected. This is a skill needed in board meetings, in marriages, and in financial dealings. So keep in mind that the future preparation is, in the final analysis, ultimately more important than the present difficulty.

Armed with this double perspective on both today and tomorrow, you can establish appropriate, consistent, and lovingly established boundaries that can make a great difference in your adolescent's present and future life.

Is It Too Late?

Many parents of teens, aware that they are in the last stage of parenting, wonder if there is still time to help their kid learn responsibility and self-control. "Maybe I should just hang on and try to get through it," they say. That is often a sign of weariness and giving up prematurely. In most cases, however, I would say that *healthy boundaries can make a significant difference.*

Remember the story of Beth and Trevor? Beth refused to give up, and because of this the story has a good ending. Beth called me a few days later, saying, "I'm sure you hate to have people ask you for advice about this sort of thing, but I would like some about Trevor."

"Well," I said, "I would probably begin by realizing that whatever you're doing now to deal with Trevor's attitude isn't working."

"That's no problem for me," said Beth. "I've tried everything anyway."

"Are you sure?" I queried. "My hunch is that the 'everything' you have tried either isn't everything, or it hasn't been done the right way, or you haven't tried long enough. Trevor doesn't seem to experience any concern about taking responsibility for his actions. In fact, you are the one talking to me about Trevor, not Trevor. So you are more concerned than he is."

Beth replied, "I don't think Trevor even remembers what he did."

"In that case," I said, "I recommend that you start doing some things that will help Trevor be more concerned about his attitudes and actions." Then I explained to her the key principles that are in this book. And over time, as Beth began to apply them, Trevor's behaviors and speech began to change for the better. He still isn't a perfect teen—whatever that is!— but his manner and actions are much healthier and more responsible.

So don't give up. At this stage in life, your teen needs an involved parent who has good boundaries.

I say this for several reasons. First, even though teens are systematically detaching from their parents and moving into the world, at some level, *they are still dependent on their parents*. They cannot function in the world on their own. Whether they recognize it, teens still need some important things from parents, such as:

- grace, unconditional love, and compassion when the teen is hurt, failing, or bewildered
- guidance concerning school, college, and career
- wisdom for how to navigate relationship problems
- help in romantic entanglements

Teens also need the safety, structure, and warmth of a loving home that offers them protection when needed.

I have talked to many young adults who have told me, "When I was a teenager, I acted like my parents had nothing to say to me. I couldn't afford to act differently. But inside, it mattered a lot what they said."

Second, *teens do not have total freedom and permission.* Part of that freedom belongs to the parents. Teens are certainly in the last stage of childhood and should be becoming more and more autonomous. But they don't yet have the rights and privileges of an adult. For example, they still need parental permission to go to certain movies and to sign off on school outings. This is good news because *a teen's need for parental permission can be leveraged to motivate her to learn responsibility.* That is why withholding privileges can be very effective. Some parents need to take back some privileges. We will discuss this important aspect later.

Third, *the time it takes to fix matters isn't necessarily the same amount of time it took for things to go wrong.* Some parents think, *I had no boundaries for fifteen years, and now I have three years left. I don't have another fifteen to do it right, so why try?* This assumes a one-to-one correspondence of ineffective-to-effective parenting.

Actually, it's not like that at all, because it's not that simple. People can take less time to change than you might think. There are other factors involved, such as the appropriateness, consistency, and intensity of your actions; the involvement of others; and the readiness of the child's internal world.

People in their seventies and eighties sometimes wake up to how they are being selfish or irresponsible. You can't predict how telling the truth and establishing healthy boundaries will affect a teen, nor can you predict when the change will occur. I have seen parents with a seventeen-year-old who would be moving out in a few weeks still make significant inroads with a rebellious and destructive attitude. Don't let your fears and discouragement limit a process of growth that God designed for your child. Sometimes the right intervention, given at the right time, with the right people, can make all the difference in the world.

But What If My Teen Doesn't Change?

Even so, let's suppose you do have a teen who is not doing well and is almost out of the house. Consider the alternative. If you give up and go into survival mode, your teen has not experienced the benefit of being around loving, truthful, and strict parents and will be that much less ready for successful adulthood. Even if your teen resisted every effort you attempted and you saw no change at all, something good has still happened. In those last months and weeks, she has experienced and internalized some events that cannot be easily shaken loose. For that brief time, love, responsibility, freedom, and consequences were applied to your teen's life in a way that was healthy and good.

As a psychologist, I have met many adults who blew off their parents' help when they were teenagers, only to remember years later what had been done. And they know at some level that that was a good way for them to live. So even if you don't see the fruit today or tomorrow, your teen will still have some memories of the way life should be lived. Take encouragement from the words of the prodigal son who finally "got it":

> "When he came to his senses, he said, 'How many of my father's hired men have food to spare, and here I am starving to death! I will set out and go back to my father and say to him: Father, I have sinned against heaven and against you. I am no longer worthy to be called your son; make me like one of your hired men.' "[3]

Don't count on getting an apology like that. Instead, *fight the good fight of setting boundaries—all the way to the last minute that your teen is in your charge.* Your investment of time and energy will not be in vain.

How to Use This Book

This book is structured in a meaningful order for parents of teens to be able to use it in the best way. As stated earlier, part 1 will help you to develop your own personal boundaries, so that you can create the best boundaries for your teen. Part 2 is a window into the mind and world of the adolescent, so that you can understand what your teen is thinking and feeling. Part 3 shows you how to set healthy boundaries with your teen. And part 4 explores specific problems that adolescents struggle with and offers tips on what you, the parent, can do about them.

If you have a specific area you are concerned about, such as alcohol, disrespect, or sex, turn to the relevant chapter in part 4. Then, when you feel you have a grasp of what to do, start reading the book from the beginning, in order to learn how to use boundaries in the most helpful way possible. In the short term, this book will help you address problems of irresponsibility. Long term, it will help you think for yourself in ways that can mature your teen.

Sometimes the issue you are dealing with will not have boundaries at the center of its solution. For example, a depressed teen who is responsible but disconnected from others may need relationship and warmth instead of boundaries. And we will present these differences here. Boundaries are a large part of just about every problem's resolution. But bear in mind that setting boundaries alone isn't enough to make you a good parent: you also need love, reality, support, wisdom, patience, and your own growth as well. If you don't have these things in your life, this book can help you find people and ways to get them. You need them for your teen, and for you.

A Confession

Before we go too much further, however, I need to inform you that, while I believe this book can help you parent your teen, Barbi and I are still living those years as this book is being written. Our sons, Ricky and Benny, are now teens. So we are still definitely in the learning curve with you. The concepts and ideas in this book are based on my own clinical and counseling experience, my study of adolescent development, my understanding of the biblical principles of growth, and my personal experience. Still, only God knows what the future will be for our sons. We hope that the end of the teen story will turn out well for them. Until then, we are trying to live out the principles you will read about. I hope and pray for our own adolescents the same thing I hope for yours: that they will be fully prepared to take on the task of functioning as adults in the adult world.

So sit down, learn these principles and tips, and start being an active force in your adolescent's world. Be active, be loving, be present, be truthful, and be consistent; in other words, *be the parent*. If you need permission to be the parent, you have it. Reality, life, and God are all on your side. Get going, and become a parent who knows, in most every difficult situation, *when to say Yes and how to say No*.

PART ONE

BE A PARENT WITH BOUNDARIES

Time is never time at all
You can never ever leave without leaving a piece of youth
And our lives are forever changed
We will never be the same.

—Smashing Pumpkins, "Tonight, Tonight"

Ask any youth worker, youth pastor, or therapist of adolescents what most influences a teen's ability to learn responsibility and self-control, and you will get the same answer: *a parent who models those qualities*. You must live what you are teaching your teen. So this part of the book will help you to develop and grow your own boundaries. It's work. But really, how can you lose by becoming free, self-controlled, and honest yourself?

CHAPTER 1

Revisit Your Own Adolescence

One night when I was seventeen, I ran my parents' Ford Fairlane station wagon as fast as it would go. It gave out on me after about two miles. It just stopped, and that was it. The engine had to be rebuilt. What was I thinking? It was a station wagon! I had to call my dad at 1:00 a.m. so he could take me home. We had the car towed the next day.

While the Fairlane tragedy isn't a good memory, I benefited from that experience. When one of my sons told me that he had lost a watch I had given him, I remembered how crummy I had felt when I had to call my own father and tell him what had happened to the Fairlane. That memory helped me understand how bad my son was feeling about losing his watch, so I just told him, "Oh, well, we'll get another and try again."

If you have a pulse, you have similar stories from your adolescence. Teens do things that are irresponsible. That is the nature of adolescence. For some of us, the teen years had some minor blips, and for others of us, they were miserable.

For the sake of your teen, remember your own adolescence. The more you can recollect how you felt and what you did then, the better a parent you will be.

Your Teen Needs You to Have a Past

Why should you unearth those days? What benefit will it bring to your adolescent? Significant ones, as we will see. Remembering can help you show your teen:

Empathy and identification. It is easy to forget how difficult the teen years can be, and parents sometimes judge teens too harshly for behaving like a teenager.

But your teen needs a parent who will connect with him and show him empathy, who can identify with what he is going through and who understands the struggle of adolescence. He needs to know that he is not alone in the fight.

Think about how much you need someone to hear you and be there for you in your everyday struggles as an adult. What if every time you screwed up, all you heard was, "What in the world are you doing? Are you trying to ruin your life?" Wouldn't it be easy to feel disheartened and give up? Your teen, whose brain is less developed than yours, is even less resilient in the face of criticism. Your support can soften the blows that will inevitably come your teen's way.

This doesn't mean that you should tell your teen lots of stories about your own adolescence. Parents often do that, thinking it's helping, when it really ends up being more for the parent than for the teen. Instead, remember those days, give them a few stories now and then, but keep most of your memories to yourself and allow them to help you identify with your teen. I have had so many teens tell me how disconnected they feel when dad tells them all the stories of his adolescence. It's much better for you to enter their world.

Nor does identifying with your teen mean you will approve of all his choices; rather, you are able to put yourself in your teen's place—even when he is being rude, self-centered, and unreasonable. When you see a little part of yourself in your adolescent, you can give him the connection he needs to mature.

Insight and wisdom. Because you have survived your own adolescence, you have access to what helped you during those turbulent years, and why. When you remember what made a difference in your life, those memories can give you insight and wisdom so that you, in turn, can provide what your teen needs.

So ask yourself these three questions:

1. Who stuck with me without giving up on me?
2. What truths helped me make sense of the world?
3. What did I learn from the consequences of my actions?

My Boy Scout troop leader, A. J. "DK" DeKeyser, spent time with me during countless meetings and trips. He encouraged me to stay in Boy Scouts when I was ready to bail. And he didn't tell my parents every bad thing I did; instead, he handled each one himself. DK is one of those people whose wisdom helped me learn persistence, and my memories of him have reminded me of the kind of parent I want to be.

Hope. All parents wonder if their teen will ever change, become responsible, or care about his or her life. Parents don't know their children's future. Yet, *because you can remember your own adolescence, you now can understand your own life and decisions.* You know that you went through tough times and made many bad decisions, but that you gradually became more connected, self-controlled, focused, and responsible. Your own years should offer you hope for your teen; you can convey that hope even when your teen is floundering.

My mother raised four kids. After I had grown up, I asked her how she made it. She told me that when she was overwhelmed with us, she would go to her own mom, who had raised six kids. Her mom would always tell her the same thing: "It's just a stage; they'll grow out of it." This helped my mom put up with us and help us get to the next stage, whatever it was.

Try to Remember ...

Even though it's not uncommon for parents to talk about how much more challenging the world is today for teens, research statistics say otherwise. For example, between 1978 and 2002, the average age for drinking alcohol for the first time went from 16.3 years to 16.2.[4] The age for smoking the first cigarette went up from 15.2 years of age to 16.1,[5] and the age for smoking marijuana for the first time went from 18.4 years of age to 17.2.[6] In 1991, 54 percent of students had had sexual intercourse. In 2003, the percentage was 46 percent.[7]

Today's parents can rest assured that many of the challenges they faced in adolescence are similar to the challenges their teens face. So, reflect back on how, as a teen, you may have struggled in the following areas, and allow those experiences to help you offer your teen compassion and help.

Conflict with and distance from your parents. Most likely, you went through a rough patch in which you thought your parents were controlling and didn't understand you. You may have been overtly defiant and had long and loud arguments with them. Or perhaps you were sneaky and did what you wanted behind their backs. Then again, you may have never disagreed with your parents and weren't able to individuate from them. If so, you likely entered into adolescence later in life, when you had already left home.

No matter when you experienced this conflict with your parents, you probably didn't enjoy the fighting or the duplicity with them. Parents are the center of a child's life, so it's always difficult for children to disconnect from them. So when you look at your teen's surly, angry face, understand that she does not enjoy the alienation any more than you do.

Relational problems. Who were your friends? Were you into sports, studies, art, music, church, or some combination of them? Remember how central your friendships were to you. They were the only world that mattered to you.

That sort of prominence probably had its downside too: cliques, arguments, broken romances, and fights. Think of how vigilant you had to be, sometimes to the point of being more concerned with who liked you than with who you liked. Think of how devastating it was when someone you trusted turned against you, and you had no way to deal with it. That is how your teen feels.

Emotional and behavioral issues. Did you ever feel depressed and very down? Lost and confused? Did you ever get high or drunk? Go further than you wanted to sexually? Experience angry outbursts that you couldn't control?

Sometimes when we think about the good old days of our teens, we whitewash the angst, negative feelings, and out-of-control behaviors that we struggled with. It's scary to do and feel things you can't manage.

Candace told me that as a teen she felt tremendous pressure to keep everyone cheered up and was unable to experience or talk about negative emotions. As a result of this, she developed a habit of sticking pins into her fingers until she bled, and says that at some level this calmed her down. No one ever found out about what she was doing. Years later she realized that sticking herself with pins was a way for her to feel on the outside the pain she couldn't experience on the inside. (Teens who cut themselves do so for similar reasons.)

When her daughter becomes angry with her, Candace uses this memory. While she always requires respect, she also feels compassion for her daughter's frustration, and she thinks, *At least she can talk to me about what she is feeling.* Candace is using her painful memories for good parenting.

Some Tips for How to Recall

If you find it hard to remember your teen years, here are some guidelines to help you recall them, in the service of developing more compassion for your teen.

Journaling. Use the exercise of writing to bring back your teen years. Start as far back in those days as you can remember. Often the act of journaling what you know will bring forth what you have forgotten.

Talking. Conversations with friends about your past will often shake loose memories. Though it's helpful, having friends from those days is not necessary. It is more important to be with someone safe, accepting, and interested in you, so that what is inside you can be revealed.

Observing the past's effect on who you have become. Our past experiences make a significant difference in the adults we are now. Look at your strengths and weaknesses, and see how they are rooted in your teen experiences.

When I was in high school, I was way too active in sports and committees. I was tired a lot because I didn't get enough sleep, and my parents told me that they thought I was getting mononucleosis. Actually, it just turned out to be fatigue. But I can still see my tendency to be too active, and I see it in my kids too.

Grieving and letting go. Most of us had a lot of fun in our teen years, as well as a lot of loss, failure, and sadness. Entering the grief process can help us learn from what happened, move on, and help our teens. You may need to get in touch with some hurts you experienced, mistakes you made, or losses you experienced. If you haven't been able to deal with these, it will hamper your ability to empathize with your teen. We can't empathize as well if our own pains haven't been resolved. But to the extent that you have let go of past pain, you are that much more able to feel deep compassion for your teen's struggle.

Give Grace, Love, and Understanding

The next time your kid is defiant or moody, try to see your teenage self in your teen's eyes. Hold the line, tell the truth, set the limits. But give your kid grace, understanding, and love, for these years aren't easy ones. Teens need parents who "get it," who haven't forgotten their own past but instead have grown from it.

GET TO KNOW YOUR TEEN

As you revisit your teen years, think about your relationship with your parents. Did you feel they wanted to understand and connect with you? If so, you know what a positive impact this can have on a kid. It not only helped you like yourself, it likely made it easier to accept their boundaries and corrections.

But if not, how did it make you feel? What difference might it have made in your life if your parents had expressed interest in understanding and connecting with you? You have the power to make that kind of difference in your teen's life, simply by getting to know him and his world. Here are some ways to do just that.

Aim to know who your teen is rather than to change your teen. *Your teen needs to know that you want a relationship because you want a relationship.* This must be primary. If your teen thinks you want to talk to him so that you can change and fix him, you are lost, and you will get either resistance or pretense.

So second-guess and check your motives at all times. Your teen will be checking your motives as well.

Listen more, lecture less. Your teen should be using a lot of the information she learned from you and trying it out. Adolescents are working on *experiencing life more than they are receiving head knowledge.* While you should always be teaching, guiding, and correcting, the focus needs to shift. Listen more and draw her out, so that you can see what she is thinking about and struggling with. Refrain from moralizing about every wrong thing you hear.

Ask questions. Ask questions that require more than "yes" and "no." Instead of asking, "How was school?" which can be answered with an "Okay," ask, "What did you do first period?" or "Tell me about the science test; what were some of the questions?" or "What is Daniel up to these days? I haven't seen him for a while."

Follow up with more questions that are based on what you have heard. For example, suppose you asked about Daniel, and you heard, "He's okay ... he had a big fight with his girlfriend." Go after the fight. Keep finding out more.

Begin with questions about facts, move to thoughts, and then to emotions. Your adolescent needs for you to know him at a heart level, not just at an event level. This opens him up to your parenting him where he truly lives. For example, you might say, "What did you think about Daniel's argument with his girlfriend? Did you agree with his side or hers?" Now you are into his thoughts and opinions. After that, you can ask, "Did you feel bad for him? Were you angry with her?" You are now helping your teen express and put words to emotions and feelings deep inside himself.

Take off the physical pressure. Don't walk up to your teen and say, "So talk to me. Now!" Instead, say, "I don't want to lose touch with how your life is going, so I'm going to need a few minutes with you several times a week, just to touch base. Doesn't need to be a long time, but enough to see how you are doing,

how we are doing, and if there's anything I can help you with."
Your teen will likely protest, but insist on this. It's important.

Rather than sitting down to talk, take some pressure off by
taking a walk, throwing a ball, or going out for an evening with just
the two of you. (I don't recommend trying to talk while watching
television or playing a video game; it's just too powerful a distraction). Create a safe space for the teen to feel okay about opening
up with you.

CHAPTER 2

Be a Boundary

The other day I overheard my kids and their friends making plans to go to a movie. It was one of those last-minute decisions that teens often make. None of them were of driving age yet, so they were trying to solve that first obstacle.

One boy, Ted, said, "How are we going to get there? The movie starts in fifteen minutes."

His friend said, "Call your mom; she's easy."

It was true. Ted's mom, Andrea, is easy. She is a loving and easy-going person who also lets herself be taken advantage of by her teens. I have seen her interrupt plans that she has had in place for weeks in order to take her kids somewhere they decided to go at the last minute.

When I told Andrea that she was known as the "easy mom," she realized that her kids needed to learn to plan ahead. Now when they ask her to do something for them at the last minute, she tells them, "Sorry, I wish you had told me earlier, but I'm doing something else. Good luck."

Andrea does more than talk the talk; she walks the walk. She models the boundaries her children need to develop, and she helps them experience the limits they need to face.

Walk the Talk

Andrea understands the bottom line of good parenting: *teens will develop self-control and responsibility to the extent that their parents have healthy boundaries.* When it comes to good parenting, who you are is more important than what you say.

All parents have at one time or another warned and threatened their teens with some consequence, only to let it go when they didn't respond. But kids learn more from what they experience than from what they hear.

This isn't to say that you shouldn't teach and talk about boundaries and house rules. They are very important. But those rules will hold little meaning unless you stand behind them and make them real.

Your teen needs to internalize your boundaries. That is, she needs to make them part of her own internal world. She will learn a powerful lesson when she loses something she loves because of a choice she has made. The more teens experience the negative consequences of their poor choices, the more internal structure and self-control they will develop.

Every time your teen experiences your external structure, you are providing something for your teen that she cannot provide for herself. Each time you go through this process, she becomes a little more aware, a little less impulsive, a little more responsible, and a little more mindful that she will control what her future looks like.

Develop Four Key Capacities

What does this look like for you, the parent? Here are some capacities, or abilities, for you to develop, if you don't already have them. They will help you to set and keep healthy limits, which then become part of your teen's character.

Definition. Definition refers to the ability to know who you are, what you want, and what you value. When you are defined, you know what you expect from your teen, and you also know what is not okay.

The nature of adolescence is to push against the parent's definition. Teens are trying to define themselves. Parents who define themselves by whatever their teens want are not helping their children. So get a "yes" and a "no," and say them. As Jesus said, "Simply let your

'Yes' be 'Yes,' and your 'No,' 'No'; anything beyond this comes from the evil one."[8]

I know when I am around defined parents because of how their kids behave. They still ask for a lot and want a lot, but they know when they have gone too far. They have had enough experiences with their parents' definition that they have learned that when Mom or Dad isn't happy, it won't be long before they aren't happy either.

Separateness. When you have a separate sense of self, you can experience your feelings and perceptions as different from your children's. Parents with separateness can stand apart from their kids' demands, anger, and behavior and are able to respond appropriately without getting caught up in the drama.

When parents aren't separate from their children, they are said to be enmeshed. They lose themselves in their kid's world and feelings. Enmeshed parents often feel responsible for their teen's unhappiness or desires, and they lose perspective and the ability to choose.

Separateness isn't about distance and disconnection from your children. Teens need parents who love them, but they also need parents who refrain from taking responsibility for their children's feelings. Parents who are separate give up the fantasy that they can make their teens happy. Instead, they get involved in making it safe for their kids to mature into people who will be happy.

Honesty. Being a boundary means being truthful with your kids and living in reality. Teens want authenticity and have a nose for that which is fake. They may not always like your honesty, but remember that it is a template for their future dealings with people.

Being honest means, among other things, directly confronting your children when they cross a line, so that they know they have crossed it. It means to avoid saying something is okay when you know in your heart it isn't. And it means helping your kids be aware of their vulnerabilities and issues, so that they don't become blindsided by them.

I remember one time in particular when I had to confront one of my sons. I said, "You can be really selfish, and it is affecting us and your friendships. I am going to be working on this with you." I felt bad about having to be so direct, but this problem wasn't going away. A few weeks later, my son was telling me about a conflict he was having with a friend. He told me, "I think part of it was that selfish thing I do."

Parents who are able to help their teens know what they are feeling are giving their children the tools they need to be able to deal safely with their emotions without getting damaged by the external world.

Persistence. It's no secret that teens try to wear down their parents. They push and push until you finally give in, drop the issue, or postpone the consequence. Sometimes parents think this shouldn't be, and they long for a kid who doesn't butt heads with them. But, as I said earlier, teens need this head butting with their parents in order to learn how to negotiate with reality.

So parents who embody boundaries are persistent. They stick with the rules and the consequences, as long as they are reasonable. And they say "no" to attempts to manipulate, wear down, or even intimidate them.

In Dr. Cloud's and my earlier book *Boundaries with Kids*, I mentioned a mentor of mine who, many years ago, told me: "Kids will run up against your decision 10,000 times. Your job is to hold the line 10,001 times." Take a deep breath, pray, call your friends, and hold that line.

God made parents to be the guard rails on the twisting road of life. You need to be strong enough for kids to crash into over and over and over again. You must stay strong, so that your teens will learn to stay on track. Guard rails get dinged up. But if they work well, they preserve the young lives that run up against them.

CHAPTER 3

Get Connected

Every neighborhood has one: the home where all the kids hang out to talk, watch television, play video games or Ping-Pong, and eat. The home away from home. My wife and I have become close with that family in our area, because we can visit our sons when we visit with the parents (just kidding).

But sometimes the "teen place" also becomes the parents' place. From time to time, our family and several others converge in this home. The teens run around together, ignoring the parents, and the parents sit at the kitchen table talking about the teens. Since the parents feel safe with each other, we swap problems and crises. I come away feeling more normal than I did when I arrived, realizing that I'm not alone.

The kids can sense our connection too. When they walk by us, they will ask, "What are you guys talking about?" One of us will say, "Your demise." "Whatever" will be the response, and off they will go.

Here is my point: *your teen needs for you to be connected to other adults in meaningful relationships.* The sooner the better. A parent who does not have some relationships at deep and significant levels is in jeopardy of not being able to set, keep, and enforce loving boundaries. So get connected—not only for yourself, but also for your teen.

A Physics Lesson

I can't overstate how important relationships are for you as a parent of a teen. It's a matter of physics, as demonstrated by this metaphor. You, the parent, are a car, and relationships are the gasoline that provide the energy and power you need to drive down the highway of life. Parenting demands a lot of energy from you when things are going well, and when your teen resists your boundaries and requirements, parenting requires even more energy. If you don't stop at the gas station to get refueled, you will soon run out of the energy required for good parenting, and you and your kids will be in trouble.

God designed us so that we need relationship and connection to survive and make it in life. All the dedication, good intentions, will power, and discipline in the world will not help you parent your teen as much as relationships with other healthy adults will. As the wise man Solomon said, "Two people can accomplish more than twice as much as one; they get a better return for their labor. If one person falls, the other can reach out and help. But people who are alone when they fall are in real trouble."[9] *As the parent of a teen, it's only a matter of time before you will fall.* You need warm bodies to be there with you and for you when this happens.

Parents who live in an emotional vacuum run the risk of accidentally putting their teens into that vacuum. If their teen is available, warm, and connecting, these parents will sometimes use him to fill up their emotional tank. When this happens, the teen is *parenting the parent.* God did not design parents and children to function like this. When the teen is the parent, he can't bring his immaturity and problems to his parents for help. Parents can't support their child if they are depending on him to be their support system. So don't look to your teen for support. Reach out for connection elsewhere.

Four Characteristics of Good Connections

You need friends who can let you be yourself, who accept your vulnerabilities, and who love you and give you grace, no matter what. They don't have to be parents of teenagers. What matters is their character and what transpires when you are with them. Some friends have the capacity to truly fill you up. Others are enjoyable, but they can't give you what you need on a deeper level.

So look for adults whose friendships will provide the following:

Grace. It's easy to condemn yourself for not parenting right. That's why you need people in your life who can give you grace. People who don't have a judging bone in their body, who will be "for" you, no matter what. Spend time with friends who will accept you, love you unconditionally, and support you, no matter how miserably you think you are failing.

You also need friends who are "unshockable," who have the capacity to hear anything about your teen and not freak out. When you have a friend like this, you will find yourself being more honest and open about what is going on at home. This openness then leads to more successful solutions.

God's greatest gift, grace, comes from him and through us. As the Bible says, grace helps us in our time of need: "Let us then approach the throne of grace with confidence, so that we may receive mercy and find grace to help us in our time of need."[10]

When you have relationships with people who have grace, you know that you don't have to have it together. You don't have to put on a happy face; you can talk about your fears and your failures as a parent. People of grace will move closer to you and not be put off by your issues.

Identification. Parents of teens sometimes feel like they are insane, living in a bizarre world that no one else inhabits. But when you find the right people, you realize that others' lives are just as crazy, and that helps.

Some people want to cheer you up, and there's nothing wrong with that. But before you get cheered up, you need to know that others identify with your difficulty, confusion, and frustration. This knowledge provides connection, encouragement, and hope.

So get connected with people who live in your world and help you experience that you aren't alone. You need to be around people who let you know that they also get too angry, let go of their boundaries, and make bad choices with their teens.

Several of my wife's and my closest friends are parents of teens who attend our church. Without planning it, we have all migrated to the same spot at Sunday services. After church, we catch up on the latest emotional drama, school problem, or even good times with our kids. I find myself looking forward to this time, because I know they know how my life feels.

Something about the universal nature of the shared chaos and craziness creates a deep empathy and identification among parents of teens. Parenting at this stage is different from other stages. Barbi and I certainly talked with other parents about kid problems when our boys were younger, but when our kids entered adolescence, we became vulnerable at a deeper level. We opened up, not only about parenting issues, but about our personal struggles too.

Guidance. Get connected with mature people who have been down your road. You'll face many decisions regarding your teen that don't have a simple answer. As you share new ideas, advice, solutions, and brainstorming, you can receive guidance and wisdom about what to do.

One of our friends recently told me, "I think you need to increase your kid's allowance."

"Really? He hasn't said that to me," I said.

"Well, I just see him borrowing money from other kids all the time and not paying them back."

I thanked her and went to my son, who admitted that he was always short on money. He hadn't said anything because he didn't want me to think he was a spendaholic. I checked around, found out what parents were giving their teens, and increased my son's allowance. I may not have known about this if my friend hadn't been in my life, and in my son's life.

Reality. Get connected with people who will keep you grounded and centered in reality. It is easy to overidentify with the teen's world and feel as tumultuous inside as your teen does. That doesn't help either of you. People who are grounded can help stabilize you.

A friend of mine told me recently that she had discovered that her son had been drinking. She confronted the situation, talked to the people involved, and enforced appropriate consequences. But she was

Boundaries with Teens

shaken and frightened. I told her, "It's a problem, no doubt about it, but I think you've taken good initiative to deal with the drinking. As much as I can tell, you're doing a great job, and your son is simply a good kid who is experimenting with drinking. I have seen you and your husband spend many, many hours of positive time with him. I have seen how he behaves at my house and when he doesn't know someone is looking. I hear what other kids and parents say about him. You're nipping this problem in the bud, and I just don't see major problems ahead." I was able to give this mom a broader perspective about her son's character than the one she was currently experiencing.

Find people who will give you reality, people who aren't black-and-white thinkers and who don't pretend to have an answer for every problem. People who live in reality can live with conflict, failure, and pain. And when you are trapped in the present crisis and can't think beyond the next ten minutes, they are able to keep the long view in perspective.

Back to God

God designed us to be connected to him. He also is your support—for you as a parent *and* for your adolescent. You need the help that only he can give as you parent your teen. Parenting a teen is likely to bring you to your knees, and that points you to heaven, where the one who created your teen is waiting to help. He understands the adolescent passage, and he knows the intricacies of these times.

When you ask God for help and support, you are relating to your teen's real and permanent parent. Your teen will leave your home at some point, but God will always be your child's real home. There is a verse in the Psalms that says, "Yet you brought me out of the womb; you made me trust in you even at my mother's breast."[11] This illustrates the profound reality at the core of all parenting: our connection with our teen, from the womb forward, is meant to guide that child into a loving, trusting relationship with God.

Value in Community

You can't parent your teen and impose boundaries all by yourself, even if you wanted to. However, as you surround your life with the right people, you will end up not wanting to do it alone anymore anyway. Community fills up our empty spaces.

Relationships are niether a luxury nor an option for parents of teens. Your teen needs you to give him love, grace, truth, and strength. And you cannot manufacture these elements. You can only receive them from outside of yourself. So if you're not connected and plugged in with others, make it the next thing you do.

GET OVER YOUR EXCUSES

Here are some common excuses I've heard from parents about why they aren't connected with others, and my response to them.

I don't like to burden people. The right people will love you more.

I should be able to do this myself. That's not how the universe runs. It runs on relationship and support, not self-sufficiency.

I am embarrassed by my teen's situation. Most parents of teens have become unflappable; reality has been thrown in our faces so much that we don't get embarrassed anymore.

I have problems trusting. Then make that a relational issue, and ask others to help you learn to trust.

I'm too busy. The more out of control your adolescent becomes because of your isolation, the busier you will get.

I don't know where I can find the kind of people you are talking about. You can find personal and supportive relationships in many places. For instance, find a healthy church that has a good teen ministry. It will likely have some sort of supportive group for parents of teens. Or ask around about a good parenting class in a church or community college, and enroll in it, or join a support group for parents of teens.

CHAPTER 4

Face Your Guilt and Fear

I wasn't there for him, so I avoided setting limits with him." Ray was talking to me about his son Brad, who had begun drinking and running with a bad crowd. However, in assuming he would solve one problem, he actually created a second problem, and now his son was worse off.

Fortunately, Ray saw the flaw in his thinking. A self-diagnosed workaholic, Ray had, from his own report, been too wrapped up in his career to connect adequately with his son. However, now that Brad's problems were serious, Ray had reprioritized his life and was making up for lost time.

I asked him, "Why did you think that not setting limits would help?"

"I know, it doesn't make sense. I think I felt guilty for not being there enough when Brad needed me. So I thought the time I did spend with him should be positive."

Guilt fueled Ray's flawed thinking, as it does for many parents. Both guilt and fear are internal emotional states that often prevent parents from setting the right boundaries that can help a teen learn responsibility. So it's important for you to understand how these emotions can affect your own parenting and what you can do to resolve them.

Guilt

Guilt is a feeling of self-condemnation over doing something that hurts your child. When parents are too harsh, let their kid down, or are absent in some way, they will often be harsh and critical with themselves. This feeling of self-judgment can be very strong and intense.

However, guilt is not a helpful emotion. Some parents mistakenly view guilt as a sign that they care about their teen. But guilt is more about the parent, because guilt centers on the parent's failures and badness rather than on the teen's difficulty and hurt. Guilt does nothing to help the teen's situation. Instead, guilt creates an obsessive pattern of thinking that cycles around, making you beat yourself up. Guilt keeps you from doing something that will make your teen mad, disappointed, or frustrated, because you want to avoid even greater and more intense guilt feelings.

If you struggle with guilt and want resolution, learn to experience *remorse* instead. Remorse, the healthy alternative to guilt, centers on the other person. Remorse is an empathic concern for the pain that your teen feels. It is also solution oriented. If you feel remorse over something you have done that has hurt your teen, your focus is on helping your teen heal from the damage you have done. The apostle Paul explained remorse in terms of the difference between *worldly sorrow* and *godly sorrow*:

> Yet now I am happy, not because you were made sorry, but because your sorrow led you to repentance. For you became sorrowful as God intended and so were not harmed in any way by us. Godly sorrow brings repentance that leads to salvation and leaves no regret, but worldly sorrow brings death.[12]

When you feel remorse toward your teen, you free yourself to be sad about what you have done and to repair the effects. When guilt doesn't weigh you down, you are free to set and keep limits with your teen, so that your child can benefit from experiencing structure, clarity, and consequences.

So face your guilt feelings. Tell yourself: *I will sometimes let my teen down. I will not always be what my child needs me to be.* Understand that this is inevitable, but don't stop there. When you do something that hurts your teen, put your focus on how this affects her, and allow yourself to feel remorse instead so that you can give her the structure and boundaries she needs. You will help your own life as well as your teen's.

That was certainly true for Ray and Brad. Ray allowed himself to feel a healthy remorse about what had happened with his son. As a result, his care for his son drove him to spend more time with him and to connect with him in ways that helped Brad feel loved and secure. Ray also established much more consistent and effective boundaries and consequences, which helped to increase his son's self-control and sense of ownership over his life.

Fear of Withdrawal of Love

Some parents fear that if they set limits, their teen will distance and detach themselves and withdraw their love from them. This fear can cause these parents to avoid boundaries at all costs, and to do their best to keep their kid connected. When this happens, it teaches teens that they can get their way and avoid limits by cutting off the love supply. These adolescents often have difficulty experiencing healthy adult relationships, because they have learned to withdraw love, as a form of emotional blackmail, until the other person caves in. You don't want this relational future for your teen.

If you are vulnerable to fear, you may have some sort of *dependency on your teen's goodwill and feelings toward you*. You may be trying to get your teen to meet your need for love and connection. If so, you are in jeopardy of not doing right by your child.

To resolve your fear of withdrawal of love, connect with other adults who will support, affirm, and encourage you, as we discussed in the last chapter. Such adults can meet your relational needs. Use their good feelings to fill the vacuum so that when your teen withdraws because of some limits you have imposed, you can tolerate the withdrawal.

When your teen withdraws, take the initiative to go after him and try to reconnect. Teens sometimes don't have the skills to pull themselves back into relationship, so they need their parents to help them. But while you are inviting your teen back into connection with you, keep your requirements and expectations intact. Your teen still needs them.

Remember that teens need a certain amount of time and space to pull away from parents—not totally away, but enough to form their own opinions, identity, and values. When you experience this withdrawal, realize it's a normal part of your teen's developmental passage. Don't personalize it. Instead, help your teen know that it's a good thing for him and that you'll be there when he wants to reconnect.

Fear of Anger

Adolescents get angry a lot. They live in protest mode, so it is second nature for them to get mad at everything in the world, especially their parents. But some parents are *conflict-phobic*—they are uncomfortable and afraid of being the object of their teen's wrath, and so they avoid setting the limits their teen needs. However, this teaches adolescents that if they throw a tantrum, they can get out of a limit. Teens who learn this will also have difficulty experiencing healthy adult relationships. To help your child avoid this relational future, you'll want to teach him to accept responsibilities in relationships without having outbursts.

Many parents who fear their teen's anger have either had little experience in dealing with anger or had some very negative experiences. Whichever the case, these parents have few tools to deal with angry people, so they avoid confronting them because it's too uncomfortable.

If this is your struggle, in addition to fearing your teen's anger, you may also fear the strength of your own anger. To resolve this fear, learn to experience and normalize anger—your own and others'—as a part of life. Make this an intentional item of growth for yourself.

You can get used to angry feelings by dealing with them in your own supportive relationships. Tell others about your discomfort with anger, and practice expressing your anger in safe relationships. Also learn how to listen while others express their anger. Instead of panicking or fearing the worst, focus on what the person has to say and then have a conversation about it. Dr. Cloud's and my book *How to Have That Difficult Conversation You've Been Avoiding*[13] may be a good resource for helping you learn how to have healthy, confrontational conversations so that you can work through your fear of anger.

Boundaries with Teens

If your teen is never angry with you, you're probably doing something wrong! So let your teen get mad at you, and stay present with her, as long as she is in some sort of control of herself. Remind yourself that when parents hold to the established limits, adolescents respond in anger. This is normal. If you can stay with your teen's anger and still love her while holding the line, she can more readily learn to give in and let go of her anger, which is a major step toward maturity. The task is to stay connected to your teen even while she is angry, and yet still hold the line. With this approach, she can more readily accept your limit and give up her angry protest of your rules.

Guilt and fear don't have to paralyze you so that you can't set limits with your teen. The more you work out your own struggles with these unhelpful emotions, the better equipped you will be to help your teen experience and accept your love and your limits.

CHAPTER 5

Be United in Your Parenting

Consider the following dialogue:

> *Mom:* "You're letting him do anything he wants."
>
> *Dad:* "You're too strict with him."
>
> *Mom:* "He needs more discipline and structure."
>
> *Dad:* "He needs more love and encouragement."
>
> *Mom:* "He's becoming irresponsible and out of control."
>
> *Dad:* "He's becoming insecure and afraid."

And you thought teenagers had conflicts! The above conversation illustrates a primary problem that results when parents can't agree on how to parent: *split parenting*. Rather than doing what they need to do for their teen—put him together—divided parents pull their teen apart.

The Goal of Good Parenting

Adolescents have many internal divisions (I address this more completely in chapter 9). When parents consistently provide teens with warmth and structure, teens become less extreme, impulsive, and moody. In other words, they begin to grow up inside, to become *integrated*. When parents help their adolescent experience both love and limits in healthy ways, they are helping her bring those internal divisions closer and closer together, until the teen herself becomes integrated and whole.

Of course, no parents agree on everything. But in the best situations, they agree on the most important things and disagree only on styles, preferences, and smaller matters. This is what God intended, but often parents get in the way of God's design.

When parents are far apart in their values and perceptions of their teen, as in the opening conversation, the teen loses out. She has no one to contain and integrate her internal divisions. Her unifying environment is also split up, so her inner conflicts remain stuck, and can get worse.

It's natural for teens to try to split their parents. In order to get something they want, they will play one parent against the other. One of our sons did this just the other night. Barbi had told him to go to bed, as he was up too late on a school night. Instead, he walked into my home office and said, "Can you listen to this song I wrote?" He knows I am into music and was hoping that I would get him out of an established limit. Barbi and I are always having to guard against our sons' attempts to divide us.

If one parent is loving but has poor boundaries, and the other has good boundaries but is not very loving, their teen will likely be undeveloped in her ability to love and to set limits. She will have difficulty being open and vulnerable, taking responsibility, and staying attached in conflict. She will struggle to work through problems. Clearly, the stakes of split parenting are high.

Guidance to Help Your Teen Come Together

If you and your spouse have significant disagreements about your teen, you can begin to resolve your conflicts—and go a long way toward maturing your child—by doing the following.

Agree that your teen comes first. Talk about your conflicting viewpoints, and agree to work on your differences by doing what's in the best interest of your teen. Your kid has to come first. Only you, the parents, can give him the tools he will need to survive. Protect your teen, and find a way to agree on love and limits.

Defer to each other's strengths. Most parents each have an area of strength. Agree that, for your teen's sake, you will defer to the strengths of the other. For example, if you have difficulty providing clear structure for your teen, you might ask your spouse for help and guidance. Or, if you can't listen and understand at the emotional levels your child needs, get your spouse involved in the conversation. Have your mate help you not only to parent better, but also to be a better person in general. This is what marriage is about.

Don't triangulate your teen. Sometimes parents will forget their role and involve their teen in their conflicts with each other. This is called *triangulation*, and it can be devastating for the teen, because triangulation keeps kids from growing or changing in healthy ways.

Triangulation leads to all kinds of problems, such as one parent indulging the teen with privileges, freedom, and gifts as a way of stealing the kid's love from the other parent. The other parent reacts by using too much strictness and discipline in order to prove the spouse's indulgent approach wrong.

If you and your spouse are triangulating, stop. Agree to work out your differences. Consult a third party—such as a friend, pastor, or counselor—if the triangulation continues.

If one is resistant, stay balanced. Parenting differences are not always 50–50, in which both sides need to meet halfway. Often the ratio is more like 70–30, because one parent is more off-balance than the other. This isn't a hopeless situation. I have seen many spouses grow through this problem because they were humble and willing to change.

However, if your spouse is off-balance and unwilling to see how this affects your teen, take action and address this issue with your spouse. Lovingly point out that your mate's parenting style is negatively affecting your teen. If your spouse remains resistant and extreme, be careful that you don't overcompensate for the imbalance. In other words, if your spouse is too strict, don't give in to the temptation to be lenient.

Your teen doesn't need two crazy parents. At least one of you needs to be integrated. So be a balanced and integrated parent. Be full of love and reality, fun and diligence, warmth and truth. If you are, your teen will be internalizing health every time she is around you. You are making "deposits" in your kid's heart and life that are sound and loving. In times to come, she will be able to draw on those deposits and use them for comfort, encouragement, wisdom, and hope.

For Your Kid's Sake

God designed parenting to be executed by a mom and a dad who love each other and their children and who support each other's parenting, make up for each other's limitations, and correct each other's mistakes. It is a very good system when it works as planned.

So work together to become united rather than divided parents. After all, you are your teen's most important guide for how life is supposed to be lived. Kids do best when their parents stand together. Give your teen what he needs.

CHAPTER 6

Be an Integrated Parent

So what's your dad like?" I asked Traci. She had been referred to me because she was lying, skipping class, and performing poorly at school.

Traci had been quiet and uncommunicative in our first few sessions, which is typical of teens, but she was talking more now. She told me, "My dad's weird. Sometimes he is the nicest person in the world. He talks to me and jokes around, and we go places and have fun. He even takes my friends with me to go shopping."

"And then?" I asked.

"And then he can be the biggest jerk. Like, he'll get wound up tight, and put me on restriction, and call my teachers to get my assignments. He won't talk to me, except to yell."

"That must be hard to deal with."

"Yeah. I hate it when he does that."

"What do you do with the changes in your dad?"

"Well, I just avoid him when he's so mean, and I hang around him when he's nice."

Unlike the split parenting we discussed in the last chapter, when two parents aren't on the same page, this father's parenting split was internal. Traci's dad was divided within himself, and this posed a problem for his daughter. She had to deal with two different and incompatible parenting approaches within the same parent: one who was loving, with few limits; and another who was unloving and overly strict.

Did you notice how Traci responded? She did not try to get more structure from the gratifying dad. Nor did she seek more gratification from the strict dad. Traci disconnected from structure and boundaries and connected to love and gratification. Her experience with her dad taught her that *strictness is bad and total gratification is good*. As a result, Traci was on her way to a life of impulsiveness, immaturity, and irresponsibility.

You Only Parent to Your Own Level of Maturity

Parents teach their children primarily through experiences, even more than through teaching and talking. But you can't provide what you don't possess. So no matter how much you love your teen, you have a built-in limitation, and it is this: *you can only parent to your own level of maturity*.

For example, Traci's dad could not set reasonable limits with her because he didn't have them for himself. So he would swing from setting strict limits with her to having no limits. Yet he sent Traci to me because she wasn't responsible and self-controlled. It didn't take rocket science to figure out that he was part of Traci's problem. He had a split inside himself, especially in the area of love and limits.

As hurtful as this kind of split parenting can be for children, many parents have this limitation. You are probably aware of your own tendencies to go along with your teen's behavior, to not respond or confront because it's too much trouble or because you don't want the conflict. Then, out of the blue, something snaps inside you, and you come out swinging, yelling, threatening—doing whatever it takes for you to express your frustration. I look at this as the "ignore and zap" parenting style: putting up with inappropriate behaviors for too long, then blowing up.

When you consider how much teens test their parents, it's easy to understand the temptation to ignore and zap. However, even though most parents ignore and zap at times—myself included—this isn't good parenting. It teaches the teen that love and limits don't go together.

Steps to Help You and Your Teen

This problem isn't the end of the world. God has provided other resources for your teen that can take her further than you can. She has another parent, adult friends, teachers, youth pastors, coaches, and the like. Even parents who aren't internally divided need to have others around them who can help them parent better.

At the same time, however, you need to be the most integrated parent you can be, for your own sake and for the sake of your teen. So if you find yourself ignoring and zapping, here are some ways to get beyond that and move into a healthier method of parenting.

Get help for yourself. Remember, you help your teen integrate love and limits by enabling him to experience integrated love and limits through his relationship with you, the parent. If you need to become more integrated, become involved with people who can help you learn to be loving and truthful. Ask a friend, pastor, or therapist to help you, or join a support group. Many churches run Boundaries groups, where integration is one of the goals. Many churches have groups that address boundary issues in relationships. These can help you put love and limits together in your own life. As you deal with your own fears of conflict—or your anger or guilt—and get connected to people who remain with you in the process, you will become more integrated inside.

Tell your teen what part of the problem is yours. She needs to know that you aren't perfect, so that she doesn't blame herself for the inconsistency and lack of connection. Take some of the burden off your teen, and tell her something like this: "I am really sorry I got so mad last night when you and I argued over your grades. I am realizing that I overlook things with you that I shouldn't, and I stuff it all, then blow up at you out of nowhere. That's not your fault; it's about me. So, while I am still holding to the consequence for those grades, I will work on my problem. I want you to let me know if I do it again."

Get your teen around adults who put love and limits together. While you are working on your own growth, bring in the cavalry.

Expose your teen to adults who can put love and limits together. He needs to experience mature people who can take his attitudes, stay connected to him, and enforce your values. Look for these people among your own family and your friends, at your teen's school, and at your church.

Write out the rules and establish accountability. If you struggle with ignoring and zapping, write down the expectations and rules of the house. When you write them down, the rules become known and agreed upon, an objective reminder to you and your teen. Writing out the rules also helps keep you more accountable to the process, so that you will enforce what you have committed to rather than saying, "I'm tired, and she's been a good kid this week, so I'll let the poor grades slide."

You may also need some "reminders with skin on," people who can help keep you structured. Ask a friend to check in with you to see if you are applying your established limits.

Give your teen connection and consistency. Do your best to give these two things, in particular, to your teen. He needs you to connect, as much as possible, with all of his own parts and feelings, and to understand and connect with his needs, rebellion, fears, disrespect, and anger. It's equally important that you be consistent. Stay the same person with your teen no matter what mood you are in.

It's easy to be attached to your adolescent when he is feeling insecure and needs your encouragement, comfort, and love. It is more of a job to connect when your teen is yelling about how much he hates you. While you should keep your limits and requirements with him, also let him know that you are "for" him, his growth, and his betterment. Talk with him about his negative behaviors without condemning him.

Why are connection and consistency such important characteristics for parents of teens? Because adolescents must have someone in their life who is strong enough to contain all of their parts—good and bad—and still relate to them. This experience enables teens to mature and become integrated. When teens don't experience connection and consistency, they can't develop a sense of self-control and responsibility. In addition, they are less able to love and accept the good and bad aspects of others. What they cannot accept in themselves, they are often not able to accept in others.

Balance Love and Responsibility

Mature adults are loving and responsible at the same time. The more you, the parent, can integrate love and limits, the better chance your teen has of internalizing them too.

CHAPTER 7

For Single Parents

If you are a single parent, you may need to know something: *you have the hardest job in the world*. You have to meet all the needs of your teen, over many years, without the help of a spouse. Some of my closest friends are single parents, and my heart breaks with theirs when they encounter the rough years of parenting. Single parenting can sometimes be brutal and overwhelming.

At the same time, many of these friends have also found the balance and resources they need, and they are experiencing success as parents. Their teens are doing well and are maturing at the right rate. So there is hope for you and your teen as well.

How to Tackle the Tough Issues

Let's take a look at the primary struggles you face as the single parent of a teen and explore what you can do to meet those challenges.

Not enough of you. Single parents have to do the work of two parents, yet they have more limited resources than two-parent families, both in quantity and in ability.

This limitation becomes more of a challenge when your kids are teenagers. They push against your authority and limits and assert their freedom in a million ways. Parents who have a spouse can hand off their teen to the other parent when they are feeling worn out. My wife and I do this all the time. But you can't do this as a single parent. If your teen doesn't let up on you, you don't get a chance to rest and regroup. This can be exhausting, and it's easy to feel you don't have any strength left inside to resist your kid's resistance.

What can you do? The answer isn't trying harder, or using your will power. Instead, realize that you don't have what you don't have. *You will need to get from the outside what you don't possess on the inside.* You need to do this for your kid, and for yourself as well.

You may need to take a break from the fracas and say, "I'm getting worn out with this, but I want to finish it. I'll get back to you." Call a safe and sane friend and get your emotional tank filled, and then enter the ring again and resolve the issue.

It's tempting for single parents to think, *I am so tired. I just don't have it in me to spend a lot of time talking with my kid. Besides, he's almost an adult anyway, so he probably doesn't even need a lot of me.* While your teen is almost an adult, he still needs bonding time with you in order for him to feel safe and loved and to help him sort out the vagaries of teen life. So get some strength from others, so that you can stay attached to your teen.

Keep in mind that you may need to ask another adult, such as a mature friend, youth pastor, or counselor, to intervene. Your teen may be able to hear things from this other person that he refuses to hear from you. Regardless, get connected.

Not only do single parents have limited quantities of emotional resources, they also have limited abilities as parents. No one parent has all the abilities to parent perfectly. No one parent can provide all of the parental "nutrients" an adolescent needs: grace, empathy, validation, structure, limits, and discipline.

So surround your teen with people who have what you don't possess. If you are a beginner in rules and consequences, make sure your adolescent spends time around an adult who is down the road further than you in this area. If you are having difficulty connecting with your teen, expose him to people who are gifted at opening him up.

Rescuing your teen from failure. I recently asked a single mom who is a good friend of mine, "What do you think is the biggest mistake single parents make?"

Without hesitating, she said, "Not allowing their teens to fail."

My friend was talking about rescuing teens from experiencing their consequences. Parents who rescue their adolescents often do so out of *guilt*. They already feel bad about their kid's situation, and often feel partially responsible that their child doesn't have two parents in the home.

As a result, single parents often indulge their teen and don't enforce the consequences that should come with attitude and behavior violations. They think, *My teen already has a strike against her. I'll make it up to her a little by being easy on her.* However, this "solution" doesn't solve the problem; it merely creates a second problem. Not only does the teen have to struggle with a broken home, it's likely she will never develop any self-control. Kids from a single-parent family need limits just as much as any kid does.

So surround yourself with guilt-busters—that is, friends who will support you when your emotions tell you you're being too mean. Cry on their shoulder, allow them to give you a reality check, and let them encourage you to love your teen and still hold the line.

I have a single-parent friend who always felt guilty whenever she grounded or took privileges away from her teens. But her kids have grown up, and they have come back to her and said, "Thanks for being strict, Mom. That's why I can keep my own marriage and job together."

Making your teen the parent. Single parenting is a lonely experience. You likely have some warm memories of what it was like to be part of a couple. The emptiness can be profound, because what you once had is no more.

Some single parents begin looking to their teen to meet their emotional needs. This is called *parentifying*, because the child has become the parent. The adolescent becomes a confidant, a sounding board, a listener, a problem solver, and someone to talk to on a Friday night. Because teens look and act like grown-ups, parents can easily fall into depending on them. This may feel good to the parent, and connection is a good thing, but your teen needs room in his head for his own development and tasks. When your kid's mind is full of your life, he is too concerned with supporting you to be able to experience and deal with his own struggles and challenges.

So gently retire your teen from that job, and find loving, solid grown-ups to support you. When parents say, "My kid is my best friend," it is more of a warning than a celebration.

Exposing a teen to your dates too soon. Sometimes parents will prematurely get their teen connected to someone they are dating. Most of the time, this is due to a desire for unity and oneness. The parents have a world that involves their date and another world that involves their children, and they want to bring those two worlds together.

There is nothing wrong with that desire. After all, God designed us for connection. However, restrain yourself for the sake of your teen. She will meet the person you are dating and get attached, as you are. Then she will begin to transfer her needs for her other parent onto your date, which is perfectly normal. Your teen also wants a unified home. But if you break up with the person, your teen's life shatters a second time. If you have multiple relationships and multiple breakups, it can harm her deeply.

While you don't need to hide the reality that you are dating (as if you could anyway), it is best not to get your teen involved with that person until it looks like the two of you are likely to get married. Just keep putting yourself in your teen's shoes, and restrain your desire for a unified family. You and your teen are creating a new, unified family, which is fine.

Parenting differences with your ex. Many divorced parents differ in their parenting values, but as I pointed out earlier, it is best if they can defer to each other's strengths.

But often a parent will notice that the child has a bad attitude or misbehaves after she has spent some time with the other parent. You can attribute some of that to the teen trying to adjust and transition between two worlds, and she needs your support and patience on that. But it may also be that your ex is not providing enough structure and consistent limits.

If this is your situation, do all you can to get your ex to agree to put your kid first and to come to an agreement on parenting values and styles. If your teen's well-being is in jeopardy, you may even have to go the legal route for his protection.

If you see some negative effects when your teen spends time with your ex, but they aren't serious enough for you to take legal action, then *be the best parent you can be*. Be balanced and integrated with love and boundaries. If your ex is a Disneyland parent, don't be the hardnose, hoping to compensate. Your teen needs to be around someone whom she can take inside of herself, who is a picture of maturity, grace, and truth. Don't try to get even with your ex. Get healthy.

Ask for Help

Finally, don't try to be strong and go it alone. Ask for help from your teen's school, your church, and your friends. Single parents need more help, and they should get more.

God has a special place for you and your teen. King David wrote about how much God wants to provide for kids who don't have both parents around: "A father to the fatherless, a defender of widows, is God in his holy dwelling."[14] Ask God for help, and he will give it to you.

CHAPTER 8

For Stepparents

Here is a guaranteed cure for being a control freak: marry someone who already has kids. It won't take you long to get over your need for control.

Stepparenting can be a wonderful experience, and I have many friends who are pulling it off successfully. But even in the best situations, stepparenting requires a lot of work.

Responsibility without Authority

Teens often dismiss stepparents as having no authority in their life, even when they live with them, which means the stepparent has responsibility without having authority. You see problems and opportunities, yet you don't have the authority to control any of them. As a result, stepparents often feel helpless.

The new stepparent tends to be more at a disadvantage than the one who has been around for several years in the teen's life. Kids take time to attach, trust, and respect. The longer you are connecting, the better your odds are. Still, even stepparents who have been around for a long time often deal with the problem of not being seen as an authority.

New stepparents are often unprepared for resistance from a spouse's children. They think that love will heal all things and that they are going to help create a new family. But reality and history can't be erased, nor should they be. Stepparents are often surprised and discouraged by the conflicts they have in their three primary relationships having to do with the adolescent: the teen, their spouse, and the other parent.

If you are experiencing some challenges in these three relationships, take heart. Let's take a look at what you can do in each of these relationships to address any stepparenting and boundary problems.

You and the Teen

It's difficult to hear a teen say, "I don't have to do what you say! You aren't my parent!" You feel like you are being put down and dismissed, and you are. But there are some things you can do to make the situation better.

Know what is going on inside the teen. Look into her heart and try to see what she is feeling. She has been through a lot in her young life. Even if the divorce was amicable, her world has been split in half. The home she was designed for, the original two-parent family, is no more. Feelings of loss, alienation, anger, helplessness, and shame always accompany this loss. Any child of divorce will verify this.

She also has a deep wish for Mom and Dad to reunite. This desire has no basis in logic or reality and a great deal of basis in her heart and her past. It is simply there, strong and intense. Most teens idealize the way things were when their parents were still married and don't conceptualize how bad they were. Your presence is an obstacle to that wish being fulfilled. It is nothing personal. In the teen's mind, you are in the way of her having her wish fulfilled. So she resists your presence by being rude, defiant, and disrespectful.

Like all teens, she naturally resists boundaries and consequences. She doesn't like structure from her biological parent, and she hates getting it from you even more. Think about it: who in their right mind would want a third person telling them what to do?

Have patience and persistence in establishing a connection. No matter how much the teen resists your being around, take a great deal of time and effort to connect with him. Do things he enjoys, and get to know his world. Blow off the disregard, at least for now. Overlook these matters in the service of the greater goal of attachment and trust. A wise proverb says, "People with good sense restrain their anger; they earn esteem by overlooking wrongs."[15]

Don't try to replace the other parent. Your teen's mind has room for only two parents. If you try to force yourself into that role, you will lose. Unless the teen tells you that she wants you to parent her, consider yourself her parent's spouse. Your role is to help her have room for an additional adult in her life.

So when you hear, "You aren't my parent," agree. Say, "You're right, I'm not." Understand that a great deal of hurt, anger, and sadness lies underneath that protest. Let it be. The teen needs time to grieve on a deep emotional level before she can accept what is. Give her time, space, and support to do that.

Bear in mind also that time plays a part here. If you have married a teen's parent soon after the divorce, the wound is fresher than if the divorce had been most of the child's life. However, even if there are many years between the divorce and your marriage, teens can still harbor a deep and unfulfilled wish for Mom and Dad to finally get together. Then this old wish gets triggered by your new presence. In either scenario, listen, be aware, and be empathic.

Let the biological parent be in charge of discipline at first. At least initially, let the parent work on boundary issues. Your job is to connect and bond with the teen. When you and your spouse agree that it's time for you to take on a disciplinary role, have your spouse tell the teen. This way the teen knows that his biological parent is behind the decision. Be sure to do this thoughtfully, so that the teen can transition into accepting your new role.

You and Your Spouse

Your spouse might be reluctant to give you any support in boundaries and consequences. It may simply be too soon, as we discussed in the last section. Or, if the other parent is still involved with the teen, he may think the teen has sufficient boundaries and consequences and that bringing you into the mix might cause territorial conflict. In addition, the other parent may not be comfortable with your abilities to set and keep limits.

Be sensitive to your spouse's needs and concerns. Attend to your spouse's concerns in this matter. Think of her position. She is now responsible for her teen, without the other parent around, and has to manage the new relationship with you and the teen. She carries a heavy burden, and she doesn't want her teen to be hurt any further.

Let your spouse know you are supportive of her parenting and that you want to play this her way. Ask how you might assist her in providing structure and goals for her teen.

Allow your spouse to experience your connection with the teen. Your spouse needs to know that you love whom he loves. Let him see you putting time in to attach with his teenager. He can be calmed by watching you do the hard work of bonding with someone who may not be very interested in you. That shows character, humility, and love.

Address any questions about parenting skills. Your spouse may be concerned that you don't have the capacities to discipline, especially if you don't have kids of your own. Tell her you would like to be entrusted with some of the parenting at some point, and ask her what abilities she might be unsure of with you. Does she think you are too harsh or reactive? Inconsistent? Unsure? If her concerns are valid, let your spouse know that you will work on it, and ask her for progress reports on your parenting style.

You and the Other Parent

If the other parent is involved with the teen, both that parent and the teen may resist any efforts from you to set boundaries and consequences. The ex's resistance can range from mild, such as complaining to your spouse, to severe, such as legal action. Granted, this is a difficult challenge, but there are things you can do to make things easier.

If the other parent is causing you problems, take these steps.

Involve your spouse. Don't deal with this situation as a vigilante. Your spouse needs to be involved, as he has more responsibility, background, and knowledge. Ask him for help, and decide as a team what your approach should be. Determine what structure your spouse and his ex are providing for their teen, and then determine your place within that.

If matters between you and the ex escalate, support your spouse, but let him be in charge. The teen is still his child, and he will need to determine what to do about the ex.

Respect the other parent. Despite any negative realities you may know about the character of the other parent, understand that she has also suffered a loss. For whatever reason, she does not have the family she once had, and the situation is probably hard for her too. Pay attention to that, and respect her feelings.

If possible, talk to the other parent about your parenting concerns. Let her know that you want to support her relationship with her child and that you know the teen needs the involvement of both of his parents in his life. Keep marriage issues and parenting issues as unrelated as possible.

Ask her about any specific discipline concerns she may have. Is she against your doing any kind of disciplining, or is she more concerned about issues such as homework, curfews, or alcohol? Be open to her input and respect her role as the teen's parent, even if you disagree with her ideas and values.

Your Place in the Family

As you put the effort and time into all three of these relationships, the time will likely come when you can gradually function as a parent with the teen. Keep in mind, however, that because of the teen's age and stage, you may never achieve that role. If so, accept what is, be involved with her as best you can, and help her mature and ready herself for adulthood. Keep her interests first in mind.

You married someone you love. One of the best ways to love your spouse is by helping him love his kids in the most supportive means possible. Give up control, be humble, and earn your place in the family.

PART TWO

UNDERSTAND THE TEENAGE WORLD

Adolescence ... can be ... the cruelest place on Earth.
It can really be heartless.

—Tori Amos

So you want your teen to be more responsible, more mature, and more respectful. We all would. But before we dive into the how-tos of boundaries and limits, enter with me into the world of adolescence.

Most of us wouldn't dream of interviewing for a new job without doing some research: asking people, checking out the operations of the targeted company on the Web, and looking up its financial data. Though it's tempting to jump right into dealing with teen problems, you need to have the bigger and broader picture of the world your teen inhabits. Otherwise, you may not understand the person you are trying to help. To a teen, being understood is everything.

CHAPTER 9

Adolescence: The Last Step before Adulthood

Barbi and I were having dinner with another couple who were also parents of teens. We were talking about the highs and lows of that endeavor, and Carolyn said, "When our kids were younger, I thought how sad I would feel when they left home for college. Now I have days when I just can't wait until our teenagers leave home!"

Carolyn obviously has some mixed feelings about her children's adolescence. She is not alone. I don't know how many parents I've talked with who have said, "The preteen years were a lot of work, but, oh my gosh, the teen years are so much more!"

Some parents see adolescence itself as a problem to be solved, a tough period to be survived, and many simply hunker down in their bunker to wait out the war. While the teen years do require a lot of work for parents, I assure you, they are not wonderful for your teen either, and for good reason. It's important for you to know what adolescence is and what your teen is going through so that you can give him the support and understanding he needs during this turbulent time in his life.

What Is Adolescence?

A time of transition and change. Adolescence is more about *what is not* than about *what is*. Adolescence is not the dependent and open-eyed

69

years of childhood. Nor is it the mature and self-directed time that adulthood is meant to be. This period in your teen's life is a mix of both life stages, and it is neither.

Most people see adolescence as encompassing the teen years, roughly from age twelve to twenty. In the main, this definition is a good starting place, but keep in mind that a young adult can look twenty-five on the outside but have the emotional maturity of a twelve-year-old.

Adolescence has also gone through an "extension" in recent years. As culture has become more complex and college more expensive, and as marriage and job responsibilities have been deferred more, many individuals in their twenties are much like the teens of a few decades ago. For example, many of them still live at home and are financially, and somewhat emotionally, dependent on their parents. So be aware that as a parent, you may need to deal with that. There are good and bad reasons for this possibility. Legitimate financial and educational issues are one thing; avoiding responsibilities and risks are another.

For the purposes of this book, however, I prefer to define adolescence as *the transitional phase of life that connects childhood to adulthood*. Adolescence differs from both childhood and adulthood. The teenage years are more about change and transitions than either of these two other stages. And because so many changes take place during adolescence, these years are also more volatile and emotional.

Your teen is going through many incredible changes that envelop many areas of her life: neurological, hormonal, emotional, social, and spiritual. *All these changes happen at the same time*, which means she has a lot to manage.

To better understand how your teen feels, imagine going to a doctor with a stomach problem and hearing him say, "You have a gastrointestinal irritation, a sinus infection, a stressful life, an emotional issue, and your friends are making the problem worse." You would be overwhelmed and unsure about what to do.

Well, this is how your teen feels every day. For example, she wakes up feeling down and cranky for no reason that she can identify. Then she can't find the right clothes before school, so she is late to the car pool and feels rushed. At school, she wonders if she'll be accepted into the girl clique and if the boys like her. At dinner, her parents don't understand anything she says. That's a bad day! Your teen is disoriented inside, and with good reason.

Good and necessary. Adolescence is not a bad patch to be lived through. Rather, adolescence is a good and necessary thing. *Adolescence is helpful for your child, and it is normal.* The more you can see and experience this, the better your boundary-setting experience will be.

Preparation for adulthood. Many parents wonder, "Why can't we just go straight from childhood to adulthood without this insane time?" A fair question. The answer is this: *your teen needs a process of time in which to let go of parental dependence and move into adult independence.* This cannot be done instantly.

Your teen needs to sift through and question what you, his parents, say and who you are so that he can identify with some parts and refuse other parts. He needs to be safe in your care while he challenges and tries out his identity, role, power, and skills.

The Bible describes what is happening to your teen in this way:

> What I am saying is that as long as the heir is a child, he is no different from a slave, although he owns the whole estate. He is subject to guardians and trustees until the time set by his father. So also, when we were children, we were in slavery under the basic principles of the world.[16]

In other words, teens are under the control of an authority until they are ready to take ownership of their own life. You, the parent, are that earthly authority. One of the primary ways that you help your teen get ready for adulthood is by establishing good boundaries, consequences, and structure.

Keep in mind that teens are divided people. That is, their insides are in conflict with each other. Their feelings and thoughts are disjointed from each other in the following aspects.

Dependence vs. independence. Teens need parents but desire total freedom from them.

Goodness vs. badness. They vacillate between being perfect and having a dark side.

Reason vs. emotion. They can use thought and judgment, then switch to feelings and impulsiveness within seconds.

Internal vs. social realities. Teens can be highly introspective, then change to being highly relational.

Family vs. friends. They connect with the home front, then swing over to their peers.

These divisions are titanic and painful. But your love and your consistent structure, in the form of boundaries, can help your teen integrate his conflicting parts and find a healthy balance.

Given the importance of this time in your teen's life, it's important for you to know what a healthy adolescence looks like.

What Does a Healthy Adolescent Look Like?

The following list is true of teens who are progressing normally through adolescence. Healthy adolescents:

Make connections. They have an emotional attachment to their parents and friends. They are not detached or withdrawn; instead, they are bonded and connected to others.

Are responsible. They perform the tasks they are supposed to: schoolwork, chores, family duties, and so on. They are generally reliable and dependable, and they don't require as much supervision as preteens do.

Accept reality. While they may be somewhat perfectionistic, idealistic, or self-absorbed, healthy adolescents can come down to earth and accept reality. They understand that they and others make mistakes and that no one is perfect.

Mess up, but not severely. They have minor scrapes, but not major accidents. They may make a lot of mistakes, but they don't have many crises.

Are oriented to the outside. They are more and more invested in their friends and the outside world than they are in their family. They are connected to both, but the outside world is gaining their heart.

Make friends with other good kids. Though you may not approve of 100 percent of what these friends do, they don't drag your teen down into behavioral or moral problems.

Develop good values. They are establishing a sound system of morals, ethics, and spiritual beliefs. You may not agree with all of the particulars, but the basics are good.

Challenge their parents. They question your authority and your opinions and want to think for themselves. They are speaking up more and testing you. But these tests aren't ripping apart your family.

Notice that a healthy adolescent can still make mistakes and have problems. Remember this, or you will go nuts. Get over any need you have for an ideal and perfect kid, and accept the reality of the teen years. It will help you enjoy this period.

Hang in There!

When teens pass through adolescence with no steps skipped and within a family context of love, understanding, and structure, they become functioning adults, ready to take on their role in the world. Adolescence may, at times, drive you and your teen crazy, but it is necessary for your teen's well-being. When parents give teens what they need during this period, these years can even be enjoyable. Just hang in there—it can be a wild ride!

CHAPTER 10

A Period of Tremendous Change

Dave was laughing as he described a recent encounter with his son Matt. "I woke up in the middle of the night, and I went to get a glass of water. When I walked by Matt's door, I could see that the light was on. I knocked, and when he said to come in, I saw that he was arranging and categorizing his music CDs. I said, 'Matt, why on earth are you playing with your music? You've got school tomorrow!' Matt looked up at me and said, 'I don't know.' I realized he was telling the truth. He had no clue why; he was just doing it."

While "I don't know" can be a teen's intentional means to shut out or provoke a grown-up, it can also be the truth. *Teens often don't know what they think or feel, because on an almost daily basis, they are becoming a different person.*

An adolescent's values, opinions, and perceptions are fluid and unpredictable. Your teen is going through several momentous changes, in several areas, simultaneously. She is in a chaotic storm of trying to figure out who she is, how she feels, and whom she loves. But if you are aware of the specific ways your adolescent is changing, you can take these developmental changes into account when you address problem behaviors and attitudes.

Adolescents go through tremendous changes in four major areas: physical, mental, personal, and social. Let's take a look at each of these.

Physical Changes

Almost overnight, your teen looks more like a grown-up than a kid. During this period, his body weight almost doubles, and his height increases by about a quarter. He quickly outgrows his clothes, becomes less coordinated in sports because he's growing so quickly, and eats monstrous amounts of food to fuel his fast-burning metabolism.

I remember when my sons' voices started changing. I got home from work and my wife's car was the only car in the driveway, so I figured no one was there but Barbi and the kids. But when I opened the door, I heard strange men's voices, and I wondered, *Did Barbi give somebody a ride home, or is a neighbor visiting?* Then I realized those sounds were coming out of my sons' heads. I would never again be the only deep voice in our home.

Even more problematic can be the sexual changes you see in your teen. During adolescence, secondary sexual characteristics emerge, triggered by estrogen in girls and testosterone in boys. All of a sudden your child is living in a body that's ready for sex and babies. Your little girl has breasts and has begun menstruation; your little boy has a different voice and body hair. It's time for you to explain to your daughter how to use feminine supplies and to talk to your son about nocturnal emissions.

Even though your teen's body is mature, his emotions are not. His insides need to catch up with his outsides. If you find this challenging, think what it must be like for your teen. This is his life and his body, after all!

So get over the awkwardness and step up to the plate. Don't avoid a frank discussion about the physical changes that take place during adolescence.

Mental Changes

Teens think and process information at more conceptual levels than they could as children. Adolescents can use abstract reasoning, make hypotheses, and use deduction. These changes help get them ready to function successfully in the adult world, where they will need to draw conclusions from information, exercise judgment, and make all decisions that they will be held accountable for having made. These changes also increase your teen's ability to challenge and argue with you. Teens can be logical, persuasive, and manipulative. Sometimes they can even be right!

Personal Changes

Adolescents are undergoing complex emotional and personal changes. They are wrestling with many conflicting urges as they move toward becoming more emotionally mature. For example, your teen:

Is both independent and dependent on you. Adolescents want to have no rules, but they also need to know their parents are on their side.

Questions the beliefs and values of your family and challenges authority. Adolescents are beginning to think more about "why" than "what" they believe. "Because I said so" no longer satisfies as an answer.

Feels more confident about dislikes than about likes. The phrase "that sucks" allows teens to dismiss events, ideas, and people, without having to make an alliance with something they do believe in.

Feels intense and extreme emotions. These strong emotions, which are important to teens, affect their judgment.

Is more invested in "today" than "tomorrow." Adolescents feel alive when they are into something right now that is meaningful to them, which makes it difficult for teens to postpone gratification.

Good parenting involves giving your teen the structure, consistency, and love she needs so that she can successfully navigate all of these emotional and personal changes.

Social Changes

The center of the adolescent's life shifts from the family to his peer group. His friends become the focus and main interest of his life. He spends more time with them, on the phone with them, and instant messaging them.

This shift can often be difficult for parents. They may feel unloved, unappreciated, or abandoned. However, this shift is part of God's plan. It gradually prepares teens to be able to connect with the outside world and join their own supportive social or family group. The Bible talks about the process of "leaving and cleaving,"[17] referring to the way in which adults leave their parents' home, physically and emotionally, so that they can cleave to their own adult home.

Teens who don't make the shift from family to friends often have difficulty with jobs, dating, and friendships after they leave home. They are still tied into the home environment and don't have the tools to function outside of it.

Developing Empathy for Your Teen

As you can see, your teen is undergoing some titanic developmental changes. Take some time to think about what that must be like for her so that you feel for what she is going through.

Here's an exercise that can help you do this. Write down every problem that you see your teen going through in a week. It doesn't matter whether the problem is of her own doing. Include school problems, family conflicts, bad habits, friendship conflicts, and the like. Then ask yourself how you would feel with that set of problems, and if you had very little skill or understanding to help you deal with them. Welcome to a week in the turbulent world of the teen.

So do your best to be a safe place for your adolescent to return to when she feels insecure or fails, and offer her plenty of patience, love, and guidance so that she will gradually make better choices as she transitions from childhood to adulthood.

CHAPTER 11

Teens Think Differently

When I was a cottage parent in a children's home, one of the teens, Jeffrey, who was smaller than the other boys, would provoke the big guys unmercifully, with poor results for himself. He would say to some huge kid, "You wanna fight, Ugly?" The other boy would hit him, and Jeffrey would withdraw and cry for a few minutes. Then he would charge out again, taunting Ugly with another challenge. Over and over again, Jeffrey bugged and annoyed the bigger boys, and always lost. I would talk to him, explain that this behavior wasn't working for him, separate him from big kids, and talk to him some more. But it took Jeffrey a long time to outgrow his wishes to be the giant killer.

Every parent has similar stories about the unreasonable and extreme behaviors and attitudes of adolescents. You probably do too. Teens are impulsive, self-centered, and irrational. They have outbursts of anger and disrespect, then in a few minutes, they swing back to love and compliance. A friend of mine once said of an adult coworker, "He doesn't think the right thoughts." The same could be said of adolescents.

Most of the time, the developmental changes we reviewed in the last chapter explain these sorts of behaviors. Yet exciting research in the fields of psychiatry and neurology shows that the brains of adolescents do differ physically. Teens think differently.

Until recently, the standard view of brain development was that its hard wiring was complete by age five or so. During a child's first five years, the brain experiences explosive growth, and the experts thought that most of the brain cells and connectors were in place by that age.

However, new research using MRI technology shows that a certain area of the teen brain goes through a second burst of development, giving teens a "second chance" when it comes to developing capacities such as judgment, impulse control, dealing with right and wrong, and rationality. Teens are still developing their ability to control emotions and use their higher thought processes.

You can probably guess which part of the teen brain has fully developed: the area that has to do with emotions, reactions, and "gut" decisions. But because they have not reached maturity in the more rational parts of their brain, adolescents go with their guts and often react without thinking. It is truly a roller coaster of highs and lows for the teen.

This research validates the need for you to be involved with and aware of your teen so you can guide and confront him as needed. He is being confronted with drinking, drugs, sex, and career decisions, but he is just not yet ready to make mature decisions on his own about these issues. His brain doesn't think the right thoughts. It just can't. Your teen needs your brain to help him.

This information may come as a relief to you. You may think, *So my kid thinks strange thoughts because his brain is just that way. Now my world makes sense.* This knowledge helps you feel not so crazy, guilty, or confused. It's good to know that in time, when your teen's brain has completely developed, his more mature thought processes will fall into place. The end result gives you hope to endure the present.

But if this information causes you to feel discouraged and think, *I'll just grit my teeth and wait it out, as there's nothing I can do to change brain cell development,* please hear me out. It's actually not true that you can't do anything. You *can* do some things to affect the development of your adolescent's brain.

Research has validated the "use it or lose it" principle. Areas of the brain that are stimulated and challenged tend to grow and develop more. Those that are neglected will be less developed. So the more you expose your teen to healthy and helpful people and experiences, the more his brain will develop. It's also true that the more you allow your teen to chill out and watch television, avoiding healthier activities, the less his brain will develop.

Research has also found that environment, including the all-important area of human interaction, affects the brain. So provide your teen with as many experiences involving love, grace, safety, structure, and correction as you can. The mind and the body are deeply and intricately connected. The involved parent can truly make a positive difference.

CHAPTER 12

Separating from Parents

Being a parent of a teen can cure a person of narcissism. When your child was born, you were the center of her world. You were special to her. Now that she is an adolescent, you have become less central. No matter what you do, she continues to invest in the outside world more than she does in the home.

This is as it should be. Teens slowly move away from their parents physically, emotionally, and spiritually. Over time, they change from being "family-centric" to being "friends-centric." Their interests and activities revolve more and more around their friends. In addition, when children enter adolescence, they begin questioning their parents' values, ideas, and beliefs and begin formulating their own. This too is as it should be. *The dependent nature of the parent-child relationship is designed to end at some point.* When your teen grows up, she will still technically be your child, but she should not relate to you in the way she did as a child. In order to become healthy, functioning adults, children must sever the ties to their parents, often transforming the relationship into a friendship.

I'll never forget the time when our family was talking about our next vacation, and our boys said, "I don't want to go if we can't take friends." My initial thought was, *Intruders on our family vacation!*

But our sons were doing exactly what they should have been doing at this point in their lives: separating from their parents.

Children can't enter the world if they have not separated from their parents. They can't be fully engaged in two worlds at once. They must be outward bound in order to learn, focus, adapt, and interact successfully in the world. Don't try to fight your teen's desire for separation, because you will surely lose, and you should. She is supposed to leave home and separate from you. You will need to accept that the world is more interesting to her than you are.

This does not mean you will be forgotten, however. Your teen will still love you, go to you for guidance, and want to keep a relationship with you. She will have internalized thousands of experiences of love, honesty, morality, safety, and wisdom from you over the years, and she will take all those experiences with her as she engages with the world. She will use them to achieve goals, find love, and make her place. Again, this is as it should be.

So the issue is not *whether* your teen should separate from you, but *how*, for there is a right way and a wrong way.

What Is the Right Way to Separate?

As a parent, you'll help your teen enormously if you know the right way to separate, because then you can help him leave home in the healthiest way possible. Let's explore the primary differences between the right way to separate and the wrong way.

Within relationship versus outside of relationship. Your teen faces a challenging task. *He needs to leave you while staying connected to you.* He needs to know he can talk to you about people, thoughts, and events that don't have anything to do with you, because he needs your grounding and support. Your "being there" plays a huge role in helping him have the necessary tools and courage to safely enter adult life.

Sometimes, however, parents resist this process, to the detriment of the teen's well-being. Some parents inhibit separation by reinforcing only those thoughts and activities that are about family closeness, and they withdraw emotionally when the teen wants to explore other things. This presents the teen with a dilemma: leave home and lose his parents, or keep his parents but stay at home. Neither choice is the best for the teen.

Other parents withdraw when the teen has a negative, angry, or different viewpoint or emotion. This too puts the teen in a no-win situation. He must keep himself and lose his parents, or lose himself and keep his parents.

So what can you do to help your teen separate the right way?

Be a supporter of your kid's extra-family world, as long as that world is one that is reasonably safe and supports your own values and beliefs.

Talk to your teen, ask questions, and make him feel like it's okay to have interests outside of you.

Stay connected, even in differences. Don't let conflicts and differences alienate you. He needs you in his world, even when he says he doesn't. For example, rather than saying, "I don't want to hear about your friends drinking," say, "Tell me what you know about who is drinking. I may not agree, but I want to know whatever you'll let me know."

Do these things and you'll help your teen remain inside the relationship and separate in the right way.

Toward versus away. Ultimately, your teen should be separating from you because she is excited and interested in the people and activities in the outside world. She is moving *toward* a good world that she can become part of. It appeals to her likes, beliefs, interests, and goals. Something else is slowly replacing you.

However, some adolescents separate from their parents for the sake of getting away. Perhaps they want to escape from a great deal of conflict in the home, or maybe they feel miserable, angry, or constantly hurt because of something going on at home.

Separating for these reasons can be developmentally devastating. When teens are more invested in getting away than in finding happiness and a good fit in the world, they risk attaching to the wrong things for the sake of escape. For example, some teens get married at a very early age because their home is so bad that they just want out. Marriage gives them that escape, but since these teens didn't live in a loving and safe home, they have difficulty creating what they didn't get. Leaving home doesn't change a miserable person into a happy person. Instead, it creates a miserable person who is on her own.

So what can you do to help your teen separate the right way in this area?

Understand that her desire to get away from you is normal. Accept that she is getting tired of your control, rules, and restrictions.

Provide her with some positive and happy experiences at home.

Work with her on establishing a reasonably happy and functional environment at home. Compromise when you can, love always, and be strict when you need to. For example, you might say, "Tammy, I don't want you to think your whole life with us is about rules and consequences. I'd like to do some things that are positive for you too. Why don't you invite a couple of friends over for Friday night, and I'll grill steaks for you and you can rent a movie."

Accept that your teen is being drawn *toward* something rather than *away* from you, and help her be as content as possible at home so that she wants to leave for the right reasons, not just to escape you.

Prepared versus unprepared. If you have ever done any financial planning, you have probably looked at savings and retirement timelines or graphs. These graphs usually have two lines. One represents your income; the other your savings. The purpose of these timelines is to help you save enough money so that you can retire and live off your savings and investments. So the two lines on the graph intersect. At that point, your income will drop, but your savings will take over, so you are okay. At least, this is the plan!

You also need a "leaving home" graph in mind for your teen. One line represents your involvement, support, and resources. You provide your teen with love, care, safety, wisdom, and structure that he cannot provide on his own. The second line represents your teen's growing independence, readiness, and maturity. Over time, the "parent" line should be dropping, and the "teen" line should be rising. As he becomes more competent, responsible, and confident, he is able to take on more and more life responsibilities and functions—and you back off. You give less advice and wait for him to ask for it. Or you warn about a problem once, then leave it be.

Ideally, the two lines should intersect in your child's late teens or early twenties. At that point, he is on his own, more or less, and can meet most of his own needs and handle his own problems. Your child is prepared and ready for life. See the graph below.

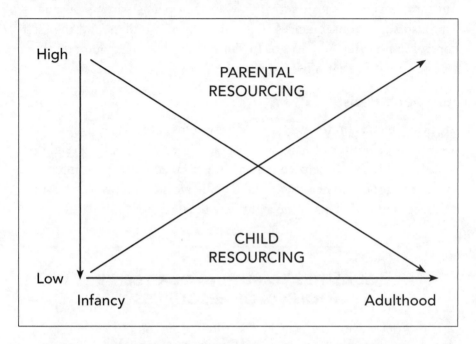

Some teens separate the wrong way in this area because, while they may be the "right" age for leaving, they are not mature enough to do so successfully. For example, perhaps they can't find and maintain healthy relationships. Or perhaps they can't control their behavior or set and achieve good goals. When teens like this leave home, it's a recipe for disaster.

So how can you help your teen be prepared to leave home?

Help him grow in his character, not just his age. Concentrate on his insides and maturity, helping him grow. Henry Cloud and I wrote a parenting book called *Raising Great Kids* in which we define character as "the sum of our abilities to deal with life as God designed us to."[18] The final goal of parenting is to equip your child with a toolbox of abilities and capabilities that will enable him to meet life's demands successfully. (See the sidebar on pages 88–89 for a list of those abilities and capacities.)

Be a parent who helps your child leave home with the optimum tools to make it in the world. For example, if your teen has angry outbursts, talk with him about those outbursts and how those may severely compromise his life. Anger can help us protect ourselves, but tantrums aren't productive. If your teen persists in his outbursts, establish some consequences that will help him understand that self-control is a better way to go. In doing this, you are equipping your teen for a world that most likely won't put up with outbursts.

Aid, Don't Resist

Yes, your teen is on the way out. Most parents are struck by how adolescence accelerates the leaving process. It goes quickly. Don't fight the separation. Instead, help your teen stay connected to you, interested in what is good and healthy in the outside world, and prepared for the challenges ahead. This is the right way to separate.

QUALITIES TO PUT IN YOUR TEEN'S TOOLBOX OF RESOURCES

Adults who successfully meet the demands of life have the following qualities:

Relational, **not alienated.** They can connect emotionally with others and have a support system of healthy people. They know when to ask for help. They can be vulnerable and open. And they can love others back, deeply and generously, in an unconditional way.

Responsible, not immature. They take ownership of their life, behavior, and attitudes, and do something good with them. They shoulder what is theirs to shoulder. They follow through. They can be relied on.

Self-controlled, not impulsive. Responsible adults make decisions based on their deliberate judgments rather than their impulses. They refrain from risky behaviors. While they can be fun and spontaneous, they make their choices count.

Values-based, not peer-driven. They have a set of standards, ethics, and beliefs that are true and transcendent. They

---

have worked out their values and follow them. Neither their peers nor the culture owns them. They are their own person.

Autonomous, not dependent. They are able to live freely and on their own. They do not need anyone else to carry them emotionally or financially. They like making their own decisions, solving their own problems, and setting their own goals.

Focused, not lost. They have found and developed their talents, passions, and gifts. They know what they want to do and what contribution they want to make with their life. They are actively engaged in that process.

Spiritual, not separated from God. They have found transcendence by learning to love, follow, and obey the Lord. They humbly trust him to take care of them, and they go to him as the source of all good things for life.

CHAPTER 13

From Earthly to Eternal Parent

When our boys were young, I was a small group leader in the children's ministry in our church. Then, when our sons moved to the junior high department, I moved with them. I remember Chris, the junior high pastor, talking to us group leaders about the difference between the faith of a child and that of a junior high kid. He said, "Before, your child's faith was his family's faith. Now he is going to be working on his faith as an individual."

Chris was right. The kids, mine included, began asking questions they had never asked in children's ministry. Some doubted the existence of God. Others thought their parents' faith was weird. Some felt that Christianity was too judgmental. Still others didn't see the relevance of faith. They were asking the right questions, at the right time. But I knew one thing for sure: gone were those "soaking-info-like-a-sponge" days of childhood. These kids were wrestling with their faith. *Hello*, adolescence!

A Time of Spiritual Wrestling

If your teen grumbles about going to church and youth group, or even declares that he doesn't believe in anything, you may be under the impression that teenagers are "on hold" spiritually, and that you had better have no spiritual expectations until your teen is a young adult. Actually, nothing could be further from the truth. The teenage years are an important spiritual time in your child's life, *whether or not he recognizes it.*

Why is this period so important? Because *your teen is in the process of changing parents.* He is transferring his dependency and obedience from you, his earthly parent, to God, his eternal parent. We were never designed to be our own authorities or judges, the absolute rulers of our lives. As adults, we are to run our destinies under God's supportive and guiding hand. The apostle Paul reminds us: "Yet for us there is but one God, the Father, from whom all things came and for whom we live."[19] The years your teen spends with you form the foundation for his true and final relationship with a parent.

Adolescence is a time of challenge and questioning in all areas, including the spiritual world. Your teen is discovering the nature and meaning of his faith. Even though it may sometimes look like it, he isn't regressing into chaos and craziness. He is going through a true and valid spiritual passage. He must go through this passage, or he will never own his faith. He must wrestle, challenge, question, and doubt so that, when he truly believes, he will have a solid and substantial faith.

How does this happen? The same way a teen does anything. He learns some information. He tests what he has learned, then decides if he truly believes it, based on that testing experience. All of us form our own life conclusions this way.

For example, children don't question the miraculous stories in the Bible. But when children become teenagers, they begin to question whether or not there was an ark, or if Jesus was raised from the dead. They doubt, argue, and say it's silly. Then they read about the Bible (I have found that teens are very interested in spiritual matters and in reading the Bible), talk to people who can talk to teens about their questions, and decide if the Christian faith is something they believe because they believe it, not because their parents have told them it's true.

This is the crux of the matter: your teen needs to wrestle with God, as the young man Jacob did, and as we all must. But the struggle must be between your teen and God, not between your teen and you. It is easy for your teen to move away from God, because he identifies God with you. But then he throws the baby out with the bathwater. So give your teen room to work out his faith, and keep him around healthy people who will do the same.

Fanning the Spark of Faith into Flames

A friend of mine told me that he used to read C. S. Lewis's Chronicles of Narnia to his young son over and over again. When I asked him why, he said, "Because I want him to see that God and I are different; then he can leave me without needing to leave God." That made all the sense in the world to me.

So if your teen is raising questions, challenges, and doubts about spiritual matters, support her in this. Ask her what she thought of the church lesson. If she tells you what the teacher said, then say, "Great, but what did you think? Did you agree? Disagree? Were you bored? How did it relate to your life and friends?" Try to stir up thought and response in her, but be careful not to take on the role of the shocked or dismayed parent if she says something negative about spiritual matters. Be real, be matter-of-fact, and be engaged.

If a teen is challenging her faith, she's putting some interest and energy into it and has some investment. This is a good thing. In contrast, the complacent and apathetic kid who goes through the motions without thinking through her faith runs the risk of abandoning it during her college and adult years. Many kids go through their spiritual adolescence later in life, when their parents are no longer there to give them support, love, wisdom, and freedom.

You may be wondering, *What if my teen has zero interest in God, church, or spiritual things?* Remember that God created your teen for a relationship with him, with a longing for him. This spark simply needs to be fanned into flame.

Take the initiative. Use your teen's interest in peers to help her connect with teens who are interested in spiritual things. Do some research to find out which church in your area has a healthy high school ministry, and take your teen there. Talk to her about spiritual matters. Draw out her questions and feelings. Require that she attend church with you; let her know this is something your family does and that she needs to participate. (Chapter 34, "God and Spirituality," offers other ideas for what you can do if your teen is struggling in this area.)

Good parenting means letting your teen move away from you spiritually while at the same time keeping her pointed toward a connection with her ultimate Father. Far better for your child to ask questions while she is living with you so that you can be in a relationship while she is working through her beliefs.

CHAPTER 14

Understanding the Differences
between Boys and Girls

Adolescence brings out the distinctions in the sexes in unmistakable ways. Biologically, the secondary sexual characteristics emerge, along with a great deal of interest in the opposite sex. Teens move from palling around with "buds" into the world of flirting, romance, and dating.

I remember my first experience of this when our boys started attending the junior high ministry. It was a large ministry, over two hundred kids, and I was a small group leader. I dropped some kids off, parked the van, and headed into the building. As it wasn't time to go inside and start, the kids were outside on the grass.

It was chaos: kids running, laughing, yelling, tumbling, wrestling, darting back and forth between small clumps of other kids. I thought I was looking at a gigantic litter of puppies. The kids looked more like high schoolers than preteens, but they definitely didn't act like high schoolers.

Beneath the chaos, I noticed a pattern. The boys and girls were engaged in very different activities. The girls clustered in groups, giggling and talking to each other behind their hands. They weren't running around; they were either standing still or walking slowly. And they were watching the boys.

The boys, on the other hand, talked less but more loudly. They yelled and did goofy physical stunts to get the girls to look at them. For these kids, it was the beginning of the eternal dance of the sexes.

While it's easy to see that the behavior of boys and girls differ, the differences go deeper than that.

Characteristic Differences between Boys and Girls

The following types of differences between girls and boys are not well-defined, so they have lots of exceptions. But in general, boys and girls differ in:

Cognitive and intellectual performance. During adolescence girls are generally more verbally advanced than boys. They can reason, conceptualize, and form ideas better. Boys, however, often have stronger competencies in the mathematical and task arenas.

Emotional expression. Girls have a more complex and intuitive emotional range than boys and can connect more successfully with feelings. They are more aware and can talk about shadings of emotions, such as slight anxiety, resentment, and wistfulness, while boys do well to know if they are scared, mad, or sad. This gender difference often carries through into adulthood.

Impulsiveness and aggression. Boys are somewhat more aggressive. They take more risks and initiative than do girls and are more impulsive. Boys are more likely to get into trouble via defiance and impulse: breaking rules, fighting, and substance problems.

Girls, on the other hand, confront less directly and are more manipulative. Their troubles lean more toward social issues, such as loyalty and betrayal, and toward inward problems, such as depression.

While these differences have to do with gender, other differences have more to do with how boys and girls relate to their parents, as we shall soon see.

How Boys and Girls Relate Differently to Mom and Dad

A baby boy is born to his mother, and after a while, he begins to move past his union with her toward the world. The first relational stop in that new world is Dad. Being male, Dad is more like the boy. So it is easier for a boy to be aggressive and launch out away from Mom. He is moving to connect with someone a lot like him and to leave behind someone unlike him.

But a baby girl has a different situation and task. She is leaving "like" to connect with "unlike," and she has to exert more work and effort to make a connection. So it is more difficult sometimes for girls to be assertive, though they usually overcome this developmental hurdle.

This dynamic repeats itself in the teen years. Adolescent boys have an easier time moving toward Dad than do girls. That's one of the reasons Dad needs to be there for his teen daughter. She needs his help in order to separate from Mom. Father-daughter outings, events, and talks are especially important during the teen years.

Gender issues are real, so here are some parenting tips to keep in mind:

If you're parenting a girl:

- Help her identify with her mother and yet be able to respectfully disagree with her.
- Help her learn how to be close to her dad, but not to be coy and seductive to get what she needs from him.
- Encourage her to be feminine, yet clear about what she wants and needs.
- Teach her that the girls who are cliquish are girls to avoid, and the girls who like her for herself are girls to hang out with.

If you're parenting a boy:

- Help him accept discipline from Mom and not see Dad as having all the power and authority.
- Help him learn to be emotionally close, affectionate, and verbal about his feelings.
- Give him healthy structures for his aggression, such as sports, scouting, and outings.
- Show him that some risks are smart and some aren't. (For example, I once jumped off a roof on a dare and was on crutches for a month.)

These two lists have some things in common, because the genders are so similar. So look at these suggestions as points of emphasis, and bear in mind that *gender is not as important as character.*

Keep Gender Issues in Perspective

The sexes are not as far apart as it may seem. Who a teen is inside makes a world of difference. These are the things that matter:

1. How connected or isolated is your teen?
2. How responsible or irresponsible?
3. How self-absorbed or others-oriented?

Do not chalk up differences to gender. This is a common mistake that leads to the assumption that things will never change. For example, I heard one parent say, "Boys are just more aggressive and girls are more passive, so let them be." But parents who "let them be" can raise a rageaholic man and a dependent woman.

Parents need to understand that character attributes can certainly change. A boy's aggression can be structured and limited so that he is loving and responsible. He can be helped to become loving, relational, and connected. A girl's aggression can be developed and encouraged so that she is decisive, forthright, and in control of her life. She can be helped to connect at deep levels in ways that bring her safety and security.

So *vive la différence* between boy and girl teens. But don't let those differences keep you from helping your teen become a full and complete person, ready to encounter life with the required set of capabilities.

CHAPTER 15

The Influence of Culture

What comes to mind when you hear the word *culture*? Art museums? Symphony concerts? Ballet? Theater? Literature? These all represent wonderful, life-enriching experiences. Now, what comes to mind when you hear the phrase "teens and culture"? It's probably not anything like your first list, is it? Many parents often think of drugs and alcohol, violence, unplanned pregnancies and abortions, and a host of other nightmares. They spend energy worrying about how to protect their kids from the influences of today's culture. Some parents feel helpless, thinking they can do nothing about the popular culture.

Know this: *your teen will interact with her culture, now or later.* Far better for her if you help empower her to deal safely with cultural influences while she is still with you rather than later, when she is on her own. You can help her become a person who will one day have a positive effect on the culture. But to do this, you need to know what the culture is saying to your teen.

Culture, briefly defined, is a set of behaviors and attitudes that a society exhibits. Media, entertainment, and advertising sources not only reflect culture; they also influence it with the powerful, and often negative, messages they send. Television, radio, video games, and the

Internet give teens easy access to cavalier messages about casual sex, substance abuse, aggressive behavior, dishonesty, and much worse.

As the buying power of teens has increased, companies have begun spending a lot of money and research in order to create messages that will influence teens to want a particular product. Teen models, actors, entertainers, and shows have become more and more the norm. In fact, some researchers believe that teens now *define the culture.*

In the past, when most teens did not have much money, culture reflected the values, tastes, and interests of grown-ups. The message to teens was—more or less—grow up and the world will be yours. The message of the culture seems to be changing to *the world is yours today, and grown-ups are on the outside.*

Another message the culture is sending to teens is that there aren't any absolutes. Right and wrong are matters of preference, and truth is whatever you think it might be. This muddies the waters of people who are trying to find God, meaning, and values in a way that is consistent with reality.

No question about it, the culture can be dangerous to your teen. She is being bombarded with information, images, and messages that are tailored for her age group, maturity, and mentality. She needs you to help her navigate through all the messages coming her way.

Don't panic. Many kids are, right now, making it through these cultural waters just fine and becoming the adults they were designed to be. This is a time for you to take wise and deliberate action so that you can help your teen keep cultural influences in the right perspective so that they become a source of great growth and creativity.

Here are some tips on how to do just that.

Be Informed

Be involved and know what messages your teen is receiving. Pay attention to respectable news articles about current cultural trends. Ask your youth pastor what is going on in your local setting. Meet with school administrators and get their perspectives. I once went to a school meeting in which the local police showed photos of recent teen drug parties with the faces blocked out. The parents were told, "These kids are from your school. You may recognize your child here." It was a true cultural wake up call.

Keep your head out of the sand. Know what messages television and music are sending to your teen. Monitor the movies and shows he watches and the websites he visits. The more you know about the media your teen interacts with, the more you can be proactive and helpful. The parent who doesn't want to see these things is abandoning his teen to deal with them without a guide.

Listen to Your Teen

Teens know a wealth of information about the culture. They can't stop talking about it. So ask your teen what is going on at her school, at the movies, and at the mall. Remember, this world is becoming more important to her than her family world; she wants to engage in whatever her friends engage in. Listen to find out what those things are. Be sure to listen without moralizing; don't overuse comments such as, "That's wrong." You'll get a lot more information from your teen if you simply listen.

Lois, a friend who has kids a little older than ours, gave my wife and me a great parenting tip not long ago. She advised Barbi to use the car pool time going to and from school, sports, or social events to find out what was going on with our sons. "If you don't talk when you're driving," Lois said, "in a few minutes they forget you are there, and you can find out all sorts of stuff you really need to know!" We have gleaned a lot of helpful information from Lois's suggestion, including which kids had parents who were gone a lot so they could drink at home and which kids were cheating on tests and how.

Be Connected

Talk with your teen about the messages he's exposed to in the culture and through his peers. Bring up drugs, sex, violence, and ethics at the dinner table. He will likely resist, but keep in mind that he is confused and trying to sort this out. Your teen needs you to be explicit, clear, and direct about your views on these matters.

You don't have to know the language to talk about these issues. Just talk using matter-of-fact language: "Hillary, I want to talk with you about sex, what it means, and what I think are the limits for you."

Be Protective

You are the adult. It's your home, and your teen is your charge. Don't be afraid to take steps to manage the flow of information. Get rid of certain channels on your cable television or lock them away from access. Install computer software that restricts sexual, violent, and otherwise negative content on the Internet. Go over the lyrics of the songs your teen buys and set standards regarding their content. Don't let your teen hang out with kids who you feel may bring her harm. Remember, teens don't have the judgment and wisdom that parents possess, so she needs you to protect her.

Know Your Teen

Some kids are more vulnerable to cultural pressures than others. Is your teen one of them? While broad-based standards are good, you will need to tailor them to your kid's particular frailties.

For example, let's say your daughter is susceptible to the values of her peer group, and you notice that many of her friends often wear inappropriate clothing. If you know your daughter is vulnerable in this area, you can work with her so that she doesn't drop her standards in order to fit in.

If you know your son is vulnerable to experimenting with drugs, you can give him more time and attention and provide him with structure and protection. He needs your strength to bolster his weak areas until they become more developed.

How can you get to know your teen? By daily observing how she responds to what life throws at her. You may even want to write down your observations about how she handles school, stress, corrections, friendships, responsibilities, failure, and success. Become a student of your teen.

Don't React

At the same time, don't have a knee-jerk "all culture is bad" reaction either, because it simply isn't. Much is going on in music, science, the arts, education, and technology that is healthy and good for your teen. Keep in mind that Martin Luther wrote his hymns with the music of the popular bar songs of his day, and today many churches are using modern music, entertainment, and sports to bring spiritual messages to teens.

So be careful not to throw out the good with the bad. For example, while it's true that the Internet has a lot of websites that are harmful, it can also be used to your teen's advantage when it comes to doing research. Help your teen understand how to use the Internet in healthy and helpful ways. She needs to develop, in relationship with you, the tools and capabilities she will need in order to stay unharmed by the World Wide Web, and to be able to use it to find her path as an adult.

Appreciate the Good, Resist the Bad

So refrain from taking an anticulture stance with your teen. Instead, teach her to have a balanced perspective of the culture, one that appreciates the good and resists the destructive. As you discuss with your teen your own positive and negative reactions to culture and listen to hers, you can guide her toward that balance.

PART THREE

SET BOUNDARIES WITH YOUR TEEN

The readiness is all.

—William Shakespeare, *Hamlet*

Teens need love, self-control, values, restraint, and a sense of responsibility for their lives. But they do not come by this without the hard work of their parents.

This section of the book will give you the tools you need to create, establish, and follow through with boundaries and limits that can mean great progress toward maturity for your teen. No matter what the issue, from school problems to bad attitudes, and no matter the severity, from minor to critical, these keys can help you think effectively about healthy boundaries and then utilize them.

CHAPTER 16

Dig beneath Your Teen's Problem

It's not working," said Brett. "Trent's grades are still bad, even after we took away the car and grounded him. It's been a month, and he's still tanking."

Brett and his wife, Teri, looked frustrated and defeated. Their son, a bright high school student, was no longer performing well at school. They had thought some restrictions would turn him around, but they had not, and they wanted to know what I thought. I told them that I didn't know what was going on either.

The consequences seemed reasonable to me, and a sufficient amount of time had passed for them to begin taking effect, so I said, "Can I talk to him myself?" Up to that point, I had been counseling with them for marital issues. But as things improved in the marriage, Brett and Teri wanted to talk about parenting matters.

They agreed, so I met with Trent later that week. When he walked into my office, I was struck by how sad and quiet he seemed. This wasn't the rebellious and defiant kid I had heard about.

As I interviewed Trent, I understood why the consequences hadn't taken hold. He was disconnected from his parents, but not in a healthy and normal way. He was disconnected because he thought neither of them knew or cared about what he felt.

"I can't talk to them," he said. "I'm having problems with my girl-friend, I'm afraid I'm not smart enough for advanced classes, and I'm giving up. But my parents just want me to try harder. They can take away the car and ground me. They can take away everything. I don't care if they don't care."

When I met with Brett and Teri later, I told them, "We need to stop thinking this is a simple underachievement problem, solved by an adequate consequence. Trent is really alienated from you, and he will never come around till we start figuring out how you can reconnect with him."

Fortunately, Brent and Teri were able to make the changes they needed. They sat down and asked Trent how he was doing. They learned to listen to him without preaching. They empathized with his struggles. They provided support and love. And Trent responded because he began to understand that they were on his team, and his academic performance improved. Trent had regained what he needed: his parents.

Do the Spade Work

Brett and Teri are not unusual. Parents often jump into a boundary-setting approach too quickly. Sometimes they are so fed up and have felt so helpless with some attitude or behavior that when they see a strategy or approach that might work, they implement it immediately. *At least I'm doing something instead of nothing*, they think. In fact, many parents will skip this section of the book and go to the next one, which targets specific issues. So if you are reading this, good for you! It can help you prevent a lot of problems.

No one can blame a parent for wanting to get some relief and resolution on a teen problem. And if there is a crisis or emergency, such as drug or violence problems, then they don't have time to do anything else for the time being.

But as a parent, you need to realize that *teen problems have a context.* Most of the time, they don't occur out of the blue. Your teen is underachieving, being disrespectful, or acting out for a reason. He needs for you to sift and dig below the surface to make sure that what-ever is done will help him solve the issue and mature into the person

God intended him to be. Be a parent who says, "Ready, aim, fire," instead of "Fire, fire, fire."

With that in mind, let's consider some of the issues that could be working below the surface of your teen's problems.

Detachment, Hurt, or Discouragement

Problems caused by irresponsibility, immaturity, defiance, self-centeredness, and impulsiveness can often be effectively addressed by enforcing consequences. However, as Trent's situation illustrates, the problem might be caused by other concerns, such as emotional detachment, hurt, or discouragement. No amount of boundary setting will work with someone whose heart is downcast. When you beat an exhausted horse to make him run faster, the only thing the beating increases is the horse's discouragement. The same thing happens when you set limits on a discouraged teen.

A detached, hurt, or discouraged teen needs to be lifted up and given grace. She needs drawing out, listening, and acceptance: "Strengthen the feeble hands, steady the knees that give way."[20] All you may need to do to resolve the problem is connect with your teen's heart. She needs for you to tell her something like this: "I haven't really been listening to you because I've been trying to stop your bad grades. I'm sorry. It seems you might just be unhappy or struggling in some other areas, and I want to know about that. Can we talk?"

This is not an all-or-nothing consideration, however. A problem can have more than one cause. Suppose a teen has an anger problem, for example, and blows up over minor matters. It may be that she is self-centered and impatient, as well as discouraged with life. If that's the case, she needs love and support for her discouragement, and structure and consequences for her self-centeredness and impatience.

Teens, like everyone, are complex beings. Get to know your teen and who she is, so that you can figure out what is driving her problem.

Medical or Emotional Conditions

Also check out any clinical problem that might be affecting your teen's behavior. Thyroid problems, fevers, epilepsy, attention deficit disorder

(ADD), attention deficit hyperactivity disorder (ADHD), depression, and anxiety can all be factors in conduct and attitude problems.

I once knew a family whose daughter refused to go to school. She wouldn't talk about why. She just stopped going. At first her parents thought she was being defiant, so they started giving her consequences. But when they took her to an adolescent therapist, they learned that she was struggling with an anxiety disorder that rendered her paralyzed from dealing with the social and academic pressures of school. With the proper counseling and the support of her parents, this teen was soon back in school and doing well.

Here are some guidelines that can help you determine when you need to seek further help:

1. Make sure your teen has had a physical exam in the last year. Even if your teen seems healthy, don't rule out a possible physical cause until he has seen a doctor.
2. If the problem doesn't get better over time with what you are doing to help, seek a professional.
3. If a problem is severe and disruptive to life, health, school, or family, seek a professional.
4. If you know and respect some parents who have found professional help to benefit them in a similar situation, consider doing the same.

A Lack of Internal Structure

Sometimes a teen's specific behaviors are more about where she is as a person. Her conduct may indicate a lack of internal structure. By "internal structure," I am referring to the ability to be organized, focused, self-controlled, and responsible.

For example, if your teen is a slave to her impulses or if she has never been disciplined, she may have several simultaneous and troubling behaviors: academic, social, attitude, and task problems. Not only will you need to attend to these specific concerns, you will also need to deal with her lack of structure. Perhaps she needs your help in learning delayed gratification, patience, self-control, respect for authority, or ways to restrain her impulses. Talk to her about the benefits of becoming patient and self-controlled. At the same time, show her how some of her problems are due to her lack of structure. Tell her, "I want to help you learn to have more self-control and responsibility, and we will do this together." Basically, that is what most of this book is about.

As you work with both the behavior and the underlying structural problems, you are helping your teen develop the internal resources she needs in order to change her behavior. Let me show you how this works. Suppose you have a teen who has outbursts of anger. You might say, "Respectful anger is okay, but yelling and disrespect aren't. So I'll help you know when you are over the line, and when you are, you will be grounded for the weekend. I want you to know how your behavior affects other people, and I want you to be able to control yourself when you are frustrated." Not only are you telling your teen what kind of anger is not acceptable, you are also giving her an opportunity to experience restraint and self-control so that she may in time develop the internal structure she needs to be able to do this on her own, without your external motivation.

Home Environment Problems

Ongoing family problems affect teens in profound ways. Their development is often dependent on being in an environment that fosters love, safety, and structure.

Major strife in a home, such as marital problems or divorce, affects the teen. He may act out as a way to send a message that he feels but cannot put his feelings into words. Structural problems in the family also cause teen issues. The fabric of the home may be damaged. For instance, a home may have an emotionally cold or detached atmosphere, rules and limits that are too harsh or unloving, or chaos and a lack of organization.

Sometimes an adolescent will react to these environment problems with negative attitudes or bad behaviors. This raises the question: Whose problem is this, the family's or the teen's? The answer, of course, is both. The family must deal with its contribution to the problems, which can then help the teen take responsibility for his own responses.

Remember, your teen's troublesome behavior did not occur in a vacuum. It may be caused by an underlying issue that will not be solved by boundaries. Other solutions may be required, such as empathy, support, or more information.

CHAPTER 17

Use the Four Anchors of Boundary Setting

I don't know if this boundary stuff really works for me," Jill told me. She was having problems with her fourteen-year-old daughter. Holly was skipping classes at school and had been caught drinking. Things were definitely headed in the wrong direction, and Jill wanted to act before it was too late.

At the advice of a friend, Jill had read *Boundaries*, the book I wrote with Dr. Henry Cloud, and she had quickly realized she had few boundaries in her life, her marriage, and her parenting. But when she tried to implement some boundaries in her life, things hadn't gone well.

"What happened?" I asked.

"Well, I sat down with Holly a few days ago, and I told her, 'Things are going to have to change around here. I'm going to set some boundaries with you. This is for your own good. You need to stop the ditching and drinking.'"

"What happened then?"

"She got mad at me. She yelled at me. Then she left the room. The next weekend she was drinking again. I guess the next step is to send her somewhere, to some adolescent rehab center—"

"Slow down, Jill. That may be in the cards, but you're ahead of yourself. I don't think you've given Holly or yourself a real go in setting boundaries. Things are bad with her, and you do need to do some-thing. But boundaries aren't about just giving someone their marching orders and then expecting them to salute. Especially teens."

"So what are you saying?"

"I'm saying I want you to do some things this week, things that need to be included whenever we set limits and establish boundaries. Try these, and let's talk next week."

Jill had thought that simply being direct and honest was all that was needed to set boundaries. But it isn't. There are other necessary elements. I explained to Jill the following information.

Every boundary-setting conversation or situation must make use of four anchoring principles. As anchors stabilize ships, these four principles can provide stability, focus, and clarity to parents who want to establish healthy and appropriate boundaries with their teen. When applied to boundary setting, these principles help parents optimize the chances for success with the teen.

As you read over these principles, remember that they apply not only to what you *say*, but also to what you *do*.

Anchor #1

Love: I Am on Your Side

Always *begin with love*. To the best of your ability, convey to your teen that you care about her welfare and have her best interests at heart.

Boundaries separate people, at least at first. Because of this, set-ting boundaries often causes conflict. Teens get mad and feel perse-cuted. They resist boundaries, because boundaries seem harsh and uncaring.

Love will help your teen hear what you are saying, accept the boundaries, and tolerate the consequences. This is true for all of us. When we hear hard truths from someone who cares about us, we need to know that the person is on our side. Otherwise, we are liable to feel hated, bad, worthless, unloved, offended, or victimized. Those feel-ings don't lead to a happy ending.

To demonstrate love to your teen, tell her something like this: "I am on your side. I am not doing this because I'm mad, or want to pun-ish you, or don't care about you. I am doing this because I want your best." You may not be feeling especially close to your teen when you set a limit, but love is greater than momentary feelings. Love is a stance, an attitude to take: you are on your teen's side and for her good.

Love also helps the teen begin to see that *her behavior is the problem, not an out-of-control and angry parent.* When you don't include love, your teen is apt to think her biggest issue is getting away from you, the upset or angry adult. Love helps the teen point to herself as the problem.

When Jill, whom you met at the beginning of the chapter, realized that all her daughter saw was an angry mom, she spent some time reflecting and talking to others about what she loved about her daughter and how deeply she wanted Holly's life to be better. The next time they talked, Jill told Holly, "I want to go over the things I'm concerned about and solve some problems. But before I go any further, I want you to know that I really do love you, and I don't want bad things for you. I want a good life for you, and that's why I want to help you with these problems."

Holly was a little hesitant because of past interactions with her mom, but she listened without getting angry or withdrawing from the rest of what Jill had to say.

Anchor #2

Truth: I Have Some Rules and Requirements

Love opens the door to change but is not enough. Truth provides guidance, wisdom, information, and correction. Truth exists in the form of rules, requirements, and expectations for your teen. They are the dos and don'ts that spell out what your teen needs to do and what he needs to avoid.

Why is this important? Because *your teen needs to know what the line is, so that he can choose whether or not to cross it.* If there is no line, you won't be able to blame your teen for crossing it. Sometimes a boundary doesn't work because the parent didn't clearly define the boundary.

By the way, if you feel weird or mean about having rules and expectations for your teens, you should see that feeling as a problem! It is not cruel and unloving for parents to have requirements for their teen's behavior and attitude. Teens who have reasonable expectations for their behavior tend to do better in life, because boundaries are part of life. Adults can't show up for work late, nor should they yell at their spouse when they've had a bad day. As long as the rules are appropriate for the situation, *when you bring them into the relationship, you are helping your child see that structure and responsibility are normal and expected in life.*

Make your rules and requirements specific and understandable. Your teen needs to know clearly what is acceptable and what is not. As a rule of thumb, the more immature your teen, the more specific you must be. For example, it's easy to get bugged at a teen who doesn't pick up his plate and silverware after a meal, rinse them off, and put them in the dishwasher. But often, parents just get mad instead of sitting down and explaining what they expect their teen to do, as well as what will happen if it doesn't get done.

Don't get mad. Get clear. Let your adolescent know what is expected and required in behavior and attitude. Write down your rules and regulations and post them on the refrigerator. Otherwise, when he feels you are being unfair in your discipline, he may be right. As Paul noted, "Where there is no law there is no transgression."[21]

For example, Jill told Holly: "I need to be clear about this, because I don't think I have been clear in the past, or I haven't been very loving about it. But I want there to be no misunderstanding. I will not tolerate your ditching school and your drinking. It is definitely not okay in our house. Whether or not you agree with that, it is the rule in this home."

Holly didn't like that, but it did help her get the message: there were now lines to be respected—or to be crossed.

Anchor #3

Freedom: You Can Choose to Respect or Reject the Rules

Most parents don't have a problem with love and truth. They make sense on an intuitive level. But they often choke on this one. *Are you kidding? Give my kid freedom? I already have enough chaos in my home. Why don't I just add some kerosene to the fire here?*

No one would blame you for asking that question. Your teen has probably exercised freedom to make some poor choices, and you haven't seen much good come from that. But freedom is absolutely necessary, for a couple of reasons:

You can't really make your teen choose the right thing. It can be scary to realize this, but realize it you must. There is a lot you can't control in your teen. You aren't present for much of her life, so you can't control what she does in school and with her friends. Nor can you really control what she does at home, if you think about it.

I recently fell into a power struggle with one of my sons. The conversation went like this:

"Okay, time to clean up your room."

"What if I don't?"

"Well, you have to."

"But what if I don't?"

"Well, you just have to."

"But you can't make me."

"Well … ummm …"

At this point, I regained my sanity and moved onto a better path.

"Yep, you're right. I can't make you. But you won't be skateboarding with your friends who are coming over until your room is clean." He grumblingly did the job.

Whenever you find yourself in the "you have to" and "I'll make you" trap, get out of it. Remember that there aren't many things we can literally force our teens to do.

Freedom to choose poorly is necessary to learn to choose well. Even if you could "make" your teen do the right thing, it wouldn't help him develop into a mature, loving, responsible person. That is not how God designed the growth process. He orchestrated things so that we must be free to choose good or bad, to choose him or reject him. That is the only way we can learn from our mistakes, and the only way we can truly love each other from the heart.

You don't want to be a robot, forced to do only right. Nor do you want that for your teen, though sometimes it is tempting. So affirm and validate the freedom he already has.

Of course, freedom has a limit. If a problem is life-threatening or dangerous, you certainly should intervene. Intervention in the form of involuntary hospitalizations, arrests, or residential treatment programs sometimes has to happen in extreme cases. You want your child alive to be able to grow. But as much as possible, affirm and protect your teen's freedom.

Jill told Holly, "I can't stop you from skipping class. I don't want to control you. I would rather you choose the right things. So unless things get dangerous, you are free to follow these house rules or not to. But [as we will deal with in the next section] remember, Holly, you may be choosing in a way that causes me to severely restrict many of your privileges. Skipping class is not okay. I can't follow you from class to class, but your freedoms here will be very, very limited if you continue this."

Holly liked that, of course. She knew she had the choice. She had been exercising it often. But Jill wisely wasn't confusing the issue with a power struggle that she would certainly lose.

Anchor #4

Reality: Here Is What Will Happen

If the only anchors were love, truth, and freedom, they would not be enough. Children raised with only these three principles can easily become out of control. A fourth anchor, *reality*, adds the necessary balance.

What is reality? Simply put, reality defines what is or what exists. For our purposes, however, I am using the word to describe what exists for the teen in the form of *consequences*. That is, if she chooses to utilize her freedom to reject the rules and cross the line, she will experience consequences.

Teens need consequences, because that's how they experience a fundamental law of life: good behavior brings good results and bad behavior brings uncomfortable results. In *Boundaries*, Dr. Henry Cloud and I call this the law of sowing and reaping, and it is based on a biblical concept: "Don't be misled. Remember that you can't ignore God and get away with it. You will always reap what you sow!"[22] Sowing hard work at school should reap good grades and privileges. Sowing laziness should reap poor grades and loss of freedoms.

Depending on the situation, your teen may need to experience something small, such as having to do extra chores at home. Or the consequence may need to be a big deal, such as grounding for a long time with few privileges. But the idea is the same: consequences teach us how to be responsible.

In chapter 19, "Consequences 101," we'll look at how to establish appropriate consequences, but for now, it's enough to say that *consequences should be both said and done.* Your teen needs to know what will happen on the other side of the line. She also needs to *experience* what is on the other side of the line.

Jill presented reality to Holly this way: "Yes, you are free to disobey our house rules. But from now on, the next time you skip a class, I will cooperate fully with the school in whatever detention they establish. On top of that, I will ground you from going out with your friends for a week per class missed. As for drinking, the next time I find that you have been doing that, I will remove all phone, computer, and television privileges for a month. If it happens again, the consequence will be worse."

Don't start trying to decide if that is too severe or too lax; we will deal with that later. For now, remember that consequences must exist, *and* you must follow through with them. If you state consequences without enforcing them, you will train your teen to ignore you, because your bark has no bite.

Following through was a stretch for Jill. She felt mean and didn't like Holly's anger. Holly did cross the line in both categories, but Jill held the line. When Holly crossed the line several more times, Jill held the line each time and followed through with the stated consequences. In the end, Jill was able to keep Holly at home, and both are doing well.

The next time you decide you need to have a boundary-setting conversation, be sure you tell your teen:

1. "I love you and am on your side."
2. "I have some rules and requirements for your behavior."
3. "You can choose to respect or reject these rules."
4. "Here is what will happen if you reject these rules."

When you use these four anchors, you are providing the stability, clarity, and motivation your teen needs to begin to learn self-control and responsibility.

CHAPTER 18

Don't Get Derailed

I recently saw a master at work. I watched Natalie, a fifteen-year-old, verbally take down her dad in an impressive victory.

I was having dinner with Glenn at his home. Natalie popped into the dining room to tell her dad that she was going out for a little while with a friend who was picking her up.

He said, "Wait a minute, you're on restriction. You can't go anywhere."

Natalie launched into several different ways to look at the situation: her dad had made exceptions before, her friend was depressed and needed her, she had learned her lesson already, and the restriction was unfair to begin with. Natalie used all the charm and personality a daughter has at her disposal with a dad.

Glenn, clearly out of his league, said, "Okay, I guess. Don't be gone past 10:00 p.m." And Natalie skipped out.

A few minutes later, Glenn said, "Well, she got me, didn't she?"

I said, "Looks like it."

If you are like most parents, this scenario sounds all too familiar. The good news is that it doesn't have to play out like this. Here are some keys to keep you on track when you begin to establish limits with your teen.

Accept Resistance as Normal

Most teens react with manipulation, arguments, anger, or defiance when their parents set limits with them. So the first thing you can do is accept that your teen will resist your efforts. Your teen wants total freedom, and you are standing in the way of that desire.

He will most likely use many strategies to derail your efforts to build character and responsibility through structure and consequences. Sometimes he might resist a rule or requirement you have. Other times, he might protest the consequence: "It's not fair that my curfew is 11 p.m." or "It's not fair that you grounded me for a week, when I missed my curfew by just a few minutes." Either way, be prepared to deal with your teen's attempts to derail you.

These aren't deliberate strategies, mind you. I don't think Natalie (or your teen) could explain what she did. It's more accurate to say that she instinctively manipulated her dad in order to reestablish all the choices and freedoms she wanted.

If setting limits and establishing consequences are new to you, you may encounter even more intense resistance. Your adolescent is unused to this world; restrictions, rules, and structures are getting in the way of what he wants. So move gradually at first. Have compassion on your teen. Change is never easy, and suddenly requiring him to live in a new way is a lot to ask of your teen.

Keep in mind that his resistance is a mix of good and bad. Manipulation isn't good, but the need to challenge and question you is. It prepares your teen to think for himself and to own his own values, feelings, and opinions. Life will test him on these matters. Better for your teen to figure out who he is and what he believes while he is still with you.

So love your teen, stay connected to him, and support that wrestling process.

Do Your Homework

Second, make sure your rule and your consequence are reasonable and appropriate. For example, before you set a curfew, think it through. Talk to sound-thinking people in your community whom you trust and who know kids. Come up with an age-appropriate time to be home on weekend nights. Do the same with the consequence. Figure out what is an appropriate penalty for curfew violation, using good sense and good people. Do your homework and don't be arbitrary or react. Your teen already has those capacities! Be the adult.

Involve Your Teen in the Rules and Consequences

When you are crafting your house rules, bring your adolescent into the process. Ask for her input and opinion on the rules and consequences. After all, it is her life. Let her participate.

Her involvement also mitigates against her blaming you for blindsiding her with unfair rules and consequences that don't take her feelings into consideration. She may not agree with all the rules and consequences, but she will know you didn't surprise her; she will know you took her input.

Be willing to negotiate on matters of preference and style, and stand firm on matters of principle. For example, suppose your daughter wants to wear a certain dress to the prom. While you shouldn't negotiate on matters such as modesty, you can make room for a style that is different from your tastes and that allows her to develop her identity as separate from you. Just giving teens space for safe differences will often resolve much of the resistance.

While negotiation is good when it keeps the teen involved, don't negotiate with your teen about ways to put off the consequences. Teens will try to do this. I remember one time in particular when one of my sons didn't get his chores and homework done before a scheduled boat outing with another family. I had told him that if he didn't finish on time, he would miss the event. When he missed the deadline, I told him, "Sorry, you're not going."

Several hours later, he asked me, "Can I have a different consequence?"

I said, "Sometimes I do negotiate. But the fact that you said this tells me that this consequence might be a pretty good one." So I told him no. In the following weeks, he had a better work ethic.

Contain, Don't Escalate, Your Teen's Reaction

Teens often lash out in anger when they are given requirements and consequences. It becomes a temper tantrum: "I hate you! You are the worst parent in the world! Grounding me for coming in just a little bit late is so unfair!"

Such a reaction makes many parents think their teen is a three-year-old again. The resistance to confrontation and truth can be extreme.

While your gut-level reaction might be to escalate to the same level as your kid, or to back off, neither is the best response. The first forces your teen into a power struggle with you, and the second conveys that the anger will keep you from setting limits. Instead, *contain* your adolescent's feelings.

What does this word mean? It refers to your ability to hear and understand your child's strong emotions from your own adult viewpoint. When you contain your child's feelings, you are "emotionally digesting" your teen's raw, strong feelings, so that they are more modulated, less intense, and more understandable.

To help you understand this concept, let's look at how mothers contain their young child's feelings. This is one of the most important tasks of a mother with her child. The young child has extremely strong, negative emotions, such as loneliness, fear, and rage, and he doesn't know what to do with them. They are so intense that in the child's mind, they get stronger and stronger, and he feels out of control. That's why a child often will escalate beyond all reason and have a meltdown. He experiences his own feelings as a confusing and scary thing, beyond himself. He doesn't have the capacity to calm himself, soothe his emotions, or talk sense to himself.

So what the child cannot do for himself, his mother does for him, until he learns the ability from her. The mother does not leave her child alone with those negative emotions, nor does she force him to stop. Instead, she stays present with his unhappiness and often holds him, quietly soothing the child until he feels better. This enables him to experience his own negative feelings safely since they have been, in a sense, "digested" by his mom.

Can you see the parallel here with your teen? His world is full of abrupt developmental changes, hormones, and feelings he doesn't understand. Those feelings can easily escalate and get out of control. But if you, as the adult, can help contain him, you will help your teen feel his own feelings, and not react to his own fears.

Containing is something you do inside yourself, in "being with" your teen. It is not what you say as much as how present you are. You are allowing yourself to experience your teen's wrath, fury, and disappointment in you. This is no small task. It takes work. Containing involves maintaining eye contact, being warm, and not being overwhelmed, defensive, or disrupted by your teen's emotion. It tells your teen, "Your anger and frustration are real, but our relationship is larger than those feelings. They don't scare me away, and they don't have to scare you either." This helps the teen feel more stable inside and more receptive to your input later.

This doesn't mean, however, that you should allow your teen to abuse or injure you. If things do escalate and don't seem to be getting resolved, you may need to spend time away from him so that things aren't so volatile, then try again later.

Listen Empathically

While containing is more about your presence with your teen and her negative emotions, empathic listening involves your feelings and words toward her. Empathic listening is the ability to hear and understand what your teen is saying from her own perspective and emotions rather than from yours. Empathy allows you to connect with her, join with her experience, and let her know that you understand how she feels, as much as possible.

We all need empathy. It is one of the greatest gifts we can give each other. It bridges gaps between people and helps them know they are not alone. For example, Jesus himself felt deep empathy for the suffering of others: "When he saw the crowds, he had compassion on them, because they were harassed and helpless, like sheep without a shepherd."[23]

To listen empathically:

1. Put your own experience on the back burner. That is, suspend your opinions and feelings to make room for you to understand your teen's experience.
2. Start with grace. Before you reach a conclusion about rightness or wrongness, be compassionate and understanding.

3. Ask yourself, "How would I feel in her situation?" Often, it helps to look at the problem in the way your teen looks at it.
4. Listen for feelings below the facts. That is, look for sadness, hurt, rejection, frustration, and other negative feelings that accompany the story.

Though your adolescent will probably deny it, she is floundering like a lost sheep. She needs your empathy and your care. It's not hard to have empathy for someone who is hurt, sad, or grieving. Nor is it too difficult to feel empathy for someone who is upset with a third party. But the real work of empathy is to have compassion on your teen when she is not hurt but enraged, and when *you are the object of her rage*. That requires some fortitude and work. How can you feel bad for someone who hates you?

Here is the answer: *let your teen have her pain and anger, and don't personalize it.* Put your experience temporarily on the back burner, and let yourself be empathic from within her world, not yours. If you practice this technique, you will find that your teen will often soften and respond better to your limits and consequences.

For example, you might say something like, "Yes, I understand that you are very angry at me right now for grounding you, and you think I'm unfair. I know you are upset and don't feel you are being treated right. Being grounded is going to be hard for you, and your friends are very important to you. I know this isn't easy at all for you. I do get that."

Your empathic listening is helping your teen feel understood so that *she can, at some point, see that the real problem is not a mean parent but her own behavior.* The more empathetically you connect with her, the less she is able to see you as harsh and unloving. This helps her open her eyes to the reality that she caused the consequence and can do something about it in the future.

Be Charm-Proof

Natalie's dad was a humble guy, and he admitted he was putty in his daughter's formidable hands. He said, "There's this little smile she gives me, and I just melt."

I saw the smile, and while I didn't have years of life with Natalie, I understood what it must be like for Natalie's dad. He felt love, warmth, connection, and protection toward his girl, and there is nothing wrong with that.

But something else was happening too. Both father and daughter were unknowingly engaging in a dance—the charm dance. This dance isn't a gender issue between dads and daughters and between moms and sons. It is also common between dads and sons and between moms and daughters. For a period of time, the parent will only be able to see the good, the vulnerable, and the innocent in the child, and will suspend any knowledge and experience of the negative and end up enabling, rescuing, or giving up limits for the teen.

What is going on? Most of the time, parents who allow their kids to charm them have a need that they are allowing the teen to meet. These parents may be lonely and need someone who is warm and kind. Or they may have lost their own sense of childhood, and the teen represents that innocence. Or they may be sad and need someone they can make happy so that they will feel happy. As a result, the parents' needs keep them from being direct and holding limits, because they fear their distant and angry teen will withhold what they need.

This dance can be devastating. I have seen teens who are addicts get extra chances, support, and money from their moms and dads with a certain look and smile. I have seen disrespectful kids who were yelling horrible things at their parents turn on the charm and walk away without any consequence. It looks innocent, but it not only derails the parent, it ultimately derails the teen's future.

If you and your teen engage in the charm dance, work on your own baggage. Find healthy ways to get your needs met rather than going to your teen to meet them. Free your child of the task of taking care of your heart. This will help you to require him to take responsibility for his choices. It will also help your teen give up being a charming manipulator of other people.

Charm will ultimately fail your teen, and it will bring him in contact with the wrong elements. Love, honesty, and responsibility will bring him much greater benefits. As the Bible says, "Charm is deceptive, and beauty is fleeting; but a [person] who fears the LORD is to be praised."[24] Love your teen enough to be invulnerable to charm but highly responsive to character. This will be a blessing to him.

Keep the Limit

It may seem counterintuitive to be soft, loving, and caring while holding a strict line. But that is the best thing you can do for your teen. Experience has no substitute, and your adolescent needs to go through the grounding, extra chores, or loss of privileges.

Why is this? Because learning, growth, and maturity involve not only getting information into our heads, but also getting experience under our belts. This is true in all phases of life. A medical student has to do a residency. An aspiring businessperson has to be an apprentice. And a teen who needs to learn that actions have consequences needs to experience those consequences.

Here's a small example of what can happen when parents start to hold the limit. When I drive our kids somewhere, the one sitting shotgun (front seat, passenger side) generally wants to play the stereo. My rule is that the kids have to ask me first. I want our sons to be polite and respectful of other people's things. If they don't ask permission, they can't touch the stereo for sixty seconds, and then they can ask again. The minute is the consequence.

When I first started this rule, my kids would impulsively grab the stereo and start working it. I would say, "Okay, the minute starts now." They would says things like, "I'm sorry, I'm sorry, okay? I was thinking about something else! This is a great CD, and I want my friends in the backseat to listen to it." (Actually, the friends couldn't care less.) And on and on.

At first, I used to say, "Okay, but just this time." But then I noticed that the stereo grabbing stayed a problem, and I had to keep warning. So finally I just said, "Sorry, you know the deal. And I don't want this argument to make it two minutes, okay?" And they would tolerate the sixty-second eternity. So far these days stereo grabbing is presently more an exception than a rule.

So if your teen is trying to get out of being grounded for breaking a specific rule, simply say, "While I know you're really upset with me, you are still grounded for a week. Start canceling plans if you've made them, and it's probably best if you start figuring out what you're going to do with your time here." Keep the limit.

Beware the Compliant Teen

Sometimes a parent will say to me, "One of my kids is a real challenge. But the other one is a good kid, and that makes things easier." I will generally respond with something like, "I can understand how much work the challenging kid is. It's good that you've got one who isn't in some crisis. But I recommend that you find out if your teen is choosing to be responsible for healthy reasons."

I am not saying obedience and compliance are bad. The teen who has good structure, self-control, and a high sense of responsibility is on his way to a successful life. But if the "good" kid never pushes against the limits, never questions, and *is more concerned and anxious about pleasing you than about knowing what he thinks and feels*, he may need your help to draw out his real self. When he agrees with what you are saying, ask, "Are you sure you really think everything I am saying is true? I want to know how you really feel, not just what you think I want you to say. Do I make it difficult sometimes for you to have a different opinion?" This gentle encouragement can help your teen safely express what he really feels and thinks.

A Living Warning

My friend Susan asked me to have lunch with her husband, Jeremy. She said he had been having trouble in his career and could use some advice. We met, and I asked him about his job problems. Jeremy gave me a long list of the many different positions he had held in several industries. I said, "That's a lot of different kinds of work. Why didn't any of them work out for you?"

"Too many rules. I just don't like rules."

"I know, rules are a pain. But I don't know any good jobs with no rules."

"I think I'll find one that will fit me."

Later, Susan filled in the picture for me. She had known Jeremy since they were young, and she said that she had seen him talk himself out of all sorts of consequences and responsibilities with his parents.

His parents had allowed Jeremy to derail them, and now Susan was reaping what they had sowed.

Keep Jeremy in mind when your teen tries to derail you from holding the line. Stay loving, fair, and focused. You don't want your child hopping from job to job, or relationship to relationship, because he can't tolerate frustration, rules, reality, or problems. Your teen desperately needs the safety of a loving structure. Give him the gift of a parent who won't be derailed.

CHAPTER 19

Consequences 101

Not long ago I took my kids and some of their friends to a major league baseball game for an outing. While we were watching the game, a young boy sitting behind us was making everyone miserable. He was out of control, loud, and rude.

His parents did try to manage him, but their efforts were ineffective. They shushed him, praised him when he was quiet, bribed him with food, and threatened to take him out of the game. Nothing worked.

Finally, one of my son's friends turned to me and said, "That guy needs some serious consequences." I made a note to myself to call his parents when I got home and congratulate them. I don't often hear that kind of thing from adolescents.

If you are like many of the parents I talk with, you often have difficulty identifying and following through with appropriate consequences for your teen. However, it's really not that difficult. Let's take a look at a few simple principles that can guide you in determining the right consequences for a problem with your teen. (See the sidebar on pages 136–139 for a list of sample consequences for specific problems.)

Remove the Desirable, Add the Undesirable

A consequence, basically, can be either *removing the desirable or adding the undesirable* to your teen's life as the result of a rule violation: for example, the removal of television privileges or the addition of extra chores.

In my experience, removing something a teen wants is usually more effective than adding something she doesn't want. This is true for several reasons. First, many kids today have more school and extracurricular demands (sports, music, theater, church, and so on) than their parents did, so they have less free time to do whatever has been added to their already busy schedule.

Second, it requires more of the parent's time and energy to supervise and monitor added responsibilities than it does to remove an activity. Although monitoring your teen all Saturday afternoon while she cleans out the garage to your standards can be a great consequence and a way for you to spend some time together, it does cost you. So before you impose a consequence that involves adding something your teen doesn't want, make sure it is worth your personal investment.

Don't Interfere with a Natural Consequence

Whenever possible, allow your teen to face a natural consequence to an undesirable behavior or attitude. Don't intervene. For example, allow your teen to

- lose a relationship as a result of being selfish;
- be kicked off a sports team for not meeting the grade point average requirement;
- spend the night at the police station after being picked up for loitering late at night;
- miss out on going to a movie as a result of having spent all his allowance.

Such consequences are powerful and effective. Best of all, all they require from you is that you get out of the way! Of course, many situations do not have a natural consequence, and in those instances, you need to apply something of your own making.

In addition, it is always a good idea to make your consequence as close to natural as possible. For example, if your teen acts out with his friends, you might ground him or restrict the time he spends with those friends. If he trashes the house, give him some added home upkeep responsibilities.

Make the Consequence Something That Matters to the Teen

A consequence must matter to the teen. She must be emotionally invested in it. She needs to want and desire what she is losing; she needs to not like what she is having to add. Otherwise, the experience doesn't count for much. If you have a loner kid who loves her music, she likely won't mind being restricted to her room with her stereo. That is why you need to know your own teen's heart, interests, and desires.

This might lead some parents to ask: *What if nothing matters?* They have tried everything, and the teen doesn't really seem to care. The behavior and attitudes do not change, and you don't see any evidence of increased self-control or awareness of how choices affect her future. If this is your situation, what might be the cause?

Your adolescent may be detached or even depressed. Her heart may be so disconnected that consequences don't matter, as in Trent's case in chapter 16. If so, you must find your child's heart before all else, and then help her reconnect to herself and to you.

Or your teen may not care much about people and activities. This is true of teens who live in the life of the mind. Since they aren't social, many of the typical consequences that are effective with teens may not matter a lot to them. But something matters to them — perhaps reading, watching TV, or being on the computer. Use these as consequences.

However, with kids who are more seriously introverted, they may need your help so that they will become more involved in life, people, and activities. Regard this as a problem, not a preference. Remember, all of us were designed to be attached to people and events. So get her into the mix. Then life will begin to matter to your teen; there will be something to lose.

Keep in mind that your teen may be engaging in a power play with you, holding out to see how far you will take this. If so, the consequences do matter to your teen, but she doesn't want you to know, either because she's so angry at you that she wants you to feel helpless, or because she is waiting you out in hopes that you will drop the consequence. In these situations, you may need to talk with your teen about her anger and try to connect and defuse things while also keeping the limit going. In time, your teen will likely become aware that she is only hurting herself, and will begin to respond.

When you do see a positive response, be sure you are warm and encouraging with your adolescent. When teens submit to a consequence, they often feel humiliated, weak, powerless, and alone, which puts them in a very vulnerable position. They need their parents' grace and comfort. So refrain from lecturing, making jokes, showing your teen that you were right, and so forth, or you may wound her during this period of frailty. Treat your teen as you'd like to be treated in a similar situation.

Have More Than One Kind of Consequence

While there is no perfect number of kinds of consequences you should have for your teen, you probably do need more than one. If your adolescent knows you will take away the phone every single time he breaks a rule, he is likely to do a cost analysis in order to figure out if he can do without the phone for a period of time. It might be worth it for the satisfaction of breaking the rule! So have a few different consequences to break up the predictability. You don't need many. *Just the right ones.*

Preserve the Good

Here's another good rule of thumb: *the best consequences matter the most, but preserve good things the teen needs.* Impose consequences that are a big deal to your teen, but don't remove activities that are good for her, such as participating in sports, taking music or art lessons, or going to youth activities at church, Boy Scouts, or Girl Scouts. These activities teach teens important lessons in discipline, cooperation, skill building, and coaching, and in so doing contribute to their growth. Far better to remove movies and video games, which are limited in their capacity to help kids grow up.

Of course, some behaviors or situations may require this sort of life surgery, because the bigger problem outweighs the value of the activity. A kid on drugs, for example, may have to drop sports so that he can attend Twelve-Step meetings or get treatment. Use judgment and get advice from wise friends if you are considering this step.

Distinguish between Misdemeanors and Felonies

How severe is too severe? How easy is too easy? You'll want to ensure that the consequences fit the violation appropriately. The time should fit the crime. When consequences are too strict, it can lead to alienation, discouragement, or increased rebellion. When they are too lenient, it can lead to increased disrespect and a lack of the desired change in the adolescent.

So *give the most lenient consequence that works*. Keep your mind on the goal, which is a heightened sense of responsibility, accountability, and self-awareness in your teen. If a more lenient consequence changes his behavior, and the change lasts over time, then you are on the right track. If it does not, and you are providing your teen with the right amounts of love, truth, and freedom, then you may want to increase the heat of the consequence over time until you see change.

Certainly, a serious offense merits a serious consequence. And if your teen does something seriously hurtful, such as violence or stealing, he should pay the price, in terms of restitution or what the law or school requires. But this is more a matter of justice and fairness than of changing behavior and attitudes. Both are important. So it is probably best to say that within the parameters of justice, whatever is most lenient *and works* is best.

This approach keeps parents from being unduly strict. As indicated above, it also gives you room to turn up the heat. If you max out too quickly, you have nowhere to go, and your teen will quickly tune you out and it can backfire on you.

A friend of mine found this out the hard way when she told her son, "You're grounded for a year," when he was disrespectful. Of course, disrespect is bad, but I thought a year was overdoing it. The son soon figured out that he no longer had much to lose, so he acted out more and his bad behavior escalated. His mom had maxed out her consequence equity too soon. She had to resolve the issue by admitting to her son that the year was a mistake and removing that consequence.

As a result her son felt that she was listening to his side a bit more, and things got better between them.

Use Rewards Strategically

Many parents wonder if they should have both reward and consequence plans. They want to include both the positive and the negative to have a balance.

Rewards are good things, but *teens shouldn't be rewarded for doing what is normally required in life*. After all, adults don't receive promotions for showing up to work on time or for avoiding jail time. Rewarding teens for doing what they should already be doing can result in their not being ready for the future. It can also contribute to an attitude of entitlement or to seeing themselves as superior to others.

Instead of rewarding teens for doing what they should, give them praise. We all need a pat on the back. But reserve rewards for something special, such as *extra results or extra effort.* When your teen makes unexpectedly good grades, does well in some endeavor, or knocks herself out in some task, give her a reward as a way of acknowledging the value of what she accomplished.

No Responsibility = No Privileges

As you try to determine the best consequences to use when your teen violates a rule of behavior or attitude, remember that what your kid wants most is to be in life and have friends; teens are very attached to things and relationships. Use this intense interest to help your teen understand that *privileges require responsibility, and they will be removed if there is irresponsibility.* In so doing, you will help your teen succeed in adult life.

A CONSEQUENCE LIST

Below are three categories of kinds of consequences that are fairly universal with teens. Use the examples to develop an appropriate consequence list for your teen.

Social access. Teens feel more real and alive with their friends, and they don't want to miss out on anything that is going on. This drive can help you as a parent.

Here are some specific ways you can limit your teen's social access:

Ground your teen. Don't allow her to leave home for social events. In some situations you might allow your teen to have friends over; in others you might not. Your teen's life is school, home, and whatever else that is good and healthy (sports, music or art lessons, church functions, and so on).

Keep in mind, though, that grounding can also ground you! Someone needs to be home to enforce the restriction. So if you are going to use grounding as a consequence, be sure you have figured out the logistics of which adult will be there too.

Restrict phone privileges. You might take away phone privileges for certain times and days or even altogether. Of course, if you take away your teen's cell phone, you'll make it more difficult to find your kid when you need to. Be sure you are willing to pay this price before you impose this consequence.

Uninstall instant messaging. Teens stay in contact with each other through IM on computers and often have several different conversations going on at one time on the screen. They love staying in contact this way. If you need to restrict IM as a consequence, there are software programs that restrict or eliminate usage. I have found that this is better than uninstalling it, as it is generally easy to reinstall. Talk to a computer expert about this.

Restrict driving privileges. If your teen drives, you have instant leverage! Use car access as a consequence. This only makes sense, as driving requires a certain level of maturity. Teens who show less maturity are more at risk of driving irresponsibly and possibly hurting themselves as well as others.

Several years ago, some friends of mine had a bright teenage daughter who lost interest in school during her senior year. They were very concerned, as she was college material. The family had an extra "beater" car that the daughter had been using, so when her grades started slipping, they took away the privilege so she was forced to get rides with friends, use her parents if they were available, and ride her bike to places.

The daughter was unhappy about this, but the consequence worked. She knew her parents were going to stick with the consequence, and she dearly loved driving. Soon her grades rose to their previous level.

Media. Next to friends, today's adolescents care about the world of media, making it another consequence category. As pointed out earlier, while the media can certainly expose kids to dangerous elements, it can also expose them to a lot of good information. So carefully monitor the media content rather than ban all of it.

Restrict access to the television. Television access should have limits anyway, in terms of time and programming. But it can be further restricted or removed completely. You may need to take the television out of your teen's bedroom if you can't lock access to it, or you may need to tell him he can't be in the doorway of the family room, hanging out while people are watching.

Restrict access to the computer for connecting, browsing, and listening to music. That is, anything except school assignments. More than ever, the computer is becoming a central part of life. Teens are incredibly proficient at using them. It can be a powerful consequence to remove access.

Remove access to music. Take away your teen's stereo, Walkman, iPod, or computer. This consequence can be challenging to impose, because there are so many ways a teen can get access to music. But music is an important part of adolescent life; it matters to teens.

Remove access to video games. Video games don't have much value beyond entertainment, and many can be destructive. It's not difficult to impose this consequence, as you can easily lock up all the video games.

The third category of consequences has to do with tasks.

Tasks. An added activity can be another effective consequence, as long as your teen doesn't want the activity and it is a good endeavor. For example:

Assign added chores. Give your child extra responsibilities around the house, such as loading and unloading the dishwasher, doing laundry, mowing the lawn, cooking meals for the family, and taking out trash.

Assign extra homework. If your adolescent would benefit from more assignments in a particular subject, contact the teacher and ask for it. This can be an effective consequence for problems in neglecting schoolwork.

Assign community service. Contact your city council and ask about any projects your teen could do, such as cleaning up a park or visiting residents in retirement centers. It may sound negative to use such worthy activities as consequences, and it's always better for teens to do these out of good motives. However, community service projects can hook teens into helping others, and these things can play a significant role in decreasing the undesirable behavior that started the whole process.

PART FOUR

ADDRESS COMMON PROBLEMS

Grandma: "How was school?"
Napoleon Dynamite: "The worst day of my life, what do you think?"

—*Napoleon Dynamite* (2004)

This final section provides an overall approach for how to address specific teen issues, some of which result from hurt or injury rather than the violation of a rule. The topics have been arranged alphabetically in order to make it easier for you to find a particular problem.

However, I recommend that you first read chapter 32, "Disrespect," because this problem often launches other problems and tends to show up first. For example, teens who disrespect their parents' values about drinking can be more prone to acting out with alcohol. So it's important for you to understand this problem and to deal with it in your teen.

In applying the insights and guidelines in this section, you'll not only be doing some problem solving, you will also be equipping your adolescent to take on the world as a mature and successful person.

Get informed and get equipped.

CHAPTER 20

Academic Problems

Make no mistake. Your kids are under more academic demands than you were. For better or for worse, the learning curve is steeper, and they have to study more than we did. Subject matters are more advanced. Projects, reports, and term papers require much more advance planning and steady work over time.

I can remember how jarred I was when my kids started bringing back homework assignments from junior high and high school. We were in a whole new world, and a much harder one.

When I saw how far ahead my kids had to be planning their reports, I called my mother and said, "What do you remember about my high school days, like how far in advance did I write reports?"

She said, "You wrote them in the car on the way to school."

That is what I remembered too. Most kids can't pull that off today.

Ironically, this increase in responsibility comes at a time when an adolescent's internal world is in chaos. Along with this increased responsibility comes an increase in pressure to do well. School matters more in these years. Your kid's grades and education will affect the path of his life. This too is ironic. Just when many teens stop caring about how well they do in school, their academic achievement matters more than ever.

These increases in responsibility and pressure often contribute to the problem of academic underachievement in adolescents.

Defining the Problem

Kids who have poor grades but lack the ability to make good grades are not underachievers. Technically, underachievement means that a student's performance is significantly below her ability. Testing can show this at a very accurate level. Underachieving kids can do better in school, but because they aren't motivated or don't have the necessary internal structure, they don't do better.

Academic underachievement may also be due to learning problems, attention deficit disorder (ADD), attention deficit hyperactivity disorder (ADHD), and emotional struggles, so have your teen evaluated to rule out these matters. (Motivation or structure issues can also play a part in these problems.)

Handling the Problem

If you've ruled out a physical or emotional condition as the cause for your teen's poor academic performance, you likely need to clarify your expectations and establish some consequences if she doesn't meet those expectations.

Here are some guidelines for how you can help your teen reach his academic potential:

Determine your teen's motivations. What matters to him enough to influence him to study hard? Some adolescents just gravitate toward studies and are more focused and diligent. They want to succeed because that is how they are wired. Others see how important these years are to their college or work success. They can tie in the future with the present. These teens don't need a lot of monitoring. They just need for you to provide a warm and study-supportive home.

But some kids don't care at all about these matters and need more help in terms of rewards and consequences. For other teens, progress reports and quarterly grades are too far in the future to really matter to them. They may need daily structures to help them stay on task; you may need to monitor the time spent on homework and the progress made.

Be careful not to require your teen to get certain grades, and then let him sink or swim. He may not have the internal organizational ability to last four or five weeks without someone helping him, and you will be setting him up for failure. Remember, the less ability your teen has inside, the more external structure and help he needs from the outside, until he has internalized that structure for himself.

So set up several kinds of external structures: help your teen stay on task by monitoring the time spent doing homework and how much he is accomplishing in each subject; get him into a study group; hire a tutor. Do what is necessary, given the need and the available resources.

Talk with your child's teachers and ask for their help. Most schools are more than happy to help involved parents. They appreciate your alliance with them. For instance, if your teen has the chronic "I don't know what my homework is" complaint, you and the teacher can work together to help your student improve in this area. You can have your teen write down the homework in every class, every day, in an assignment notebook. Then, at the end of class, have him go to the teacher to review it and initial it so that you know your teen has correctly written down the assignments.

Determine standards, rewards, and consequences. Set out with your teen what his grade requirements and goals are. It helps to have three levels:

1. Not okay: substandard grades, which will involve a consequence
2. Okay: acceptable grades, which will result in neither a consequence nor a reward
3. Excellent: indicating extra performance, which will involve a reward

Then determine specific rewards and consequences for grades, which can range from monetary and privilege rewards to consequences, such as loss of media, decreased social time, and increased chores. Write down what you agree to, and post the list on the refrigerator. You may need to refer to this list often. Besides, when it's in plain view, your teen will be less likely to argue with you about those rewards and consequences.

Also let your teen know that good grades are important. For example, say, "I know you don't enjoy doing homework. It's work, and I didn't like it either. But it is part of your responsibility, and I expect at least okay grades from you. I want you to succeed, and I will provide as much support as I can, but you must do the work."

Most schools give progress reports halfway between either quarter or semester reports. These reports give you objective information and time to help your teen with subjects she may be struggling with.

If grades are a problem with your teen, she likely has an unrealistic view of her success and of what is required. So don't believe her perception that she has done her work or has studied enough. Check it, check it, check it.

Establish a daily structure. If you find your teen doesn't get to homework until late or not at all, set up his after-school day so that he has to get to his assignments early enough. For example, allow him about thirty minutes to chill out when he gets home from school. Then tell him it's time to study. He can't watch television, be on the phone, listen to music, or play video and computer games until he has done the work, including home chores. You want your teen to learn to postpone having fun until *after* he has earned it. If he fools around and doesn't get to the homework until bedtime, it's straight to bed when he's finished. You are the guardian of the schedule and of his sleep routine.

Weekends should involve some study time too. Teens need weekends to relax and be with friends, but schools often assign homework over the weekend. Remember there are two, not three, weekend nights. Sunday is a technically a school night, so it's not a late night.

You Can Do It!

If your teen needs a lot of structure, you may have to put more personal time into her studying than you thought. This may be difficult if both parents work outside the home, if you are a single parent, or if you have lots of kids. But even so, your teen's needs don't change. She still needs people, support, and structure. Check with other sources, such as the school, a church, or a tutoring service to see if they can provide someone to help your teen stay on task. While a parent is ideal, anyone caring and competent can help.

Finally, your teen's lack of motivation or defiance may be beyond your resources. If that is the case, look into taking her out of the school she is in and putting her in one that is more suitable for kids who need extra structure. I have had friends with bright but unmotivated kids who have done this, and it has worked well. When the grades came back up, the kids could return to their former school. The structure helped, and so did the desire to get back in school with their friends. Military schools can also make a difference with kids who can't be reached any other way.

Don't let your teen put her future at risk simply because she's unmotivated or lacks structure. Help her change things around by providing what she needs, even if it means going an extra mile or two.

CHAPTER 21

Aggressive Behavior

What can be more upsetting to a parent than to have your own kid, who is now living in an adult body, be physically aggressive against you or someone else? Behavior like this is both surreal and frightening. Kids are supposed to be smaller and weaker than their parents so that the parents can protect them. What tables have been turned upside down so that you must now protect yourself from your child?

Defining the Problem

Unfortunately, aggression in teens has become a significant problem. Violence in the form of fighting and bullying occurs in schools, neighborhoods, public arenas, and sports stadiums. Aggressive behavior in adolescents ranges from the not so severe, such as yelling or throwing items, to the extremely severe and dangerous, such as the Columbine tragedy. While boys perform the majority of aggressive acts, girls are also becoming more aggressive. These are not excuses, for not all teens are overaggressive. Rather, these are realities you must be aware of.

The problem is understandable when you look at the factors involved: a body almost as strong as an adult's; raging emotions difficult to harness; the adolescent urge to push against all limits; and cultural and peer acceptance of violence. It's like striking a match to kerosene.

A lot of aggression occurs when parents aren't around, and you can't monitor your teen when you aren't around. So, in addition to intervening directly when your teen is aggressive in your presence, you will also need to do as much prevention as possible and to set up workable consequences and helps for those times you find out about the aggressiveness.

Left to their own devices, aggressive teens don't mature into balanced grown-ups. They risk becoming raging adults, with all the relational and career problems that go along with that. You will most likely have to do some things that your teen won't like. But the good news is that you can have a significant impact, helping your adolescent resolve and mature past hurtful behaviors.

Handling the Problem

What to do with aggression? You *must* act. Here are some guiding principles.

Draw a line. You must not be vague about aggression. The aggressive teen is pushing against limits, and often is unaware, or unconcerned, about what is okay and what is not. The more aggressive and out of control the teen, the stricter and clearer you must be.

Be clear with your teen that aggressive behavior is unacceptable and will not be tolerated. For example, you should ban:

- yelling at an adult
- throwing things
- hitting and other forms of physical aggression
- threatening violence
- taking intimidating physical stances (getting in someone's face with threatening gestures)
- carrying weapons

Establish clear consequences. Most aggressive behavior is impulsive rather than thought out. For that reason, you don't solve the problem by simply explaining to teens why you don't want them being violent. They will likely need to experience negative consequences, which will, in turn, build in them a future orientation of "What will happen next time I do this?"

So let your teen know that any aggressive behavior will result in strict limits. Be very frank in your discussion. In general, aggressive teens aren't highly aware of or concerned about their problem, so they need to know without question what will happen to them when they behave aggressively. For example, you might say, "I know I haven't followed through on your fighting before, but I've changed. The next time it happens, I will ground you, without television, computer, or music, for a month. And there will be no negotiation. This is the only warning you will get. This must stop."

Deal with retaliation. You will often get the question, "What if someone hits me first? Can't I defend myself?" This can be a trick question. Is your teen truly asking about self-defense or for permission to fight back simply because "the other guy started it"?

Be sure you clearly tell your teen that she should not let herself be injured. If she is in real physical danger and can't get away (the other kid is pursuing, she is trapped, other kids won't let her go, and so on), she should protect herself, doing what is needed to keep the other person away, but not trying to bring that person harm. This is the higher road and will help your teen distinguish between self-protection and revenge.

Barring that, however, tell your teen to walk away from fights. This is important for several reasons. It teaches self-control and helps her experience making individual choices that are probably against her peers' wishes to see a fight. Most of all, it helps your teen learn that problems can be solved in ways other than fighting.

Normalize grief and loss. Adolescents often feel they are more powerful than they really are. I am constantly amused when I watch movies with teens that involve a character fighting several bad guys against impossible odds. Invariably, one of the guys will say, "I could take those guys on, no problem." Young kids and adults rarely say something like that. But teens think they are omnipotent and are always testing the limits of their power.

Your job, however, is to help your teen integrate his power with reality. He may be stronger than he used to be as a little kid, but he isn't strong enough to win every time. If he thinks that, he is not ready for the world of adulthood, where he needs to know how to lose well and grieve well. Grown-ups know how to do their best; yet when they fail or are mistreated, they know how to feel sorrow, let things go, and move on. Sadness, fear, grief, and loss are friends, though the teen often avoids these emotions.

You can help your adolescent develop these capacities by drawing out his feelings of helplessness, fear, and sadness. Say, "It seems like you get angry and aggressive when you are facing a difficult problem or feel disappointed, like the other day when I saw you feel put down by Scott and you just went off on him. I wonder if underneath the anger, you sometimes feel scared or helpless. I certainly have those times. Do you ever have those feelings?" Such words make it normal and acceptable for your teen to experience these less powerful emotions.

You can also give your teen perspective. For example, say, "You don't have to win or come out on top all the time. Sometimes people have to accept that unfair and wrong things happen and move on. I don't feel any differently toward you when you feel sad, disappointed, or one down or inferior. In fact, I'd like to know when you feel that way." Kids who have a safe place to experience these softer emotions stand a greater chance of avoiding anger management problems later in life.

Encourage good aggression. You don't want to remove all aggression from your teen. Aggression, in its broadest sense, is simply *initiative*. It is taking active steps toward some goal. God designed each of us to learn to take initiative. Your teen is supposed to take steps to find and maintain good relationships rather than expecting others to come to him. She should learn to solve her own problems rather than waiting for someone else to do it, and to discover her own passions, talents, and gifts and invest them in the world rather than having someone tell her who to be. Aggression can help your teen find her way in the world.

However, she doesn't need to aggressively intimidate, hurt, or control others. Nor does she need to act out in rage when she is disappointed. This does her no good, now or later.

So affirm and validate good aggression. Be supportive when your teen is full of energy and somewhat goofy, or when she says things off the top of her head that she hasn't really thought about, or when she takes some risk to solve a problem. Keep helping her develop good aggression, and keep setting limits on bad aggression.

Bring the aggression into your relationship. Aggressive behavior often happens when the teen is alienated, disconnected from others, and the aggression unfortunately serves to alienate him further. Your teen's aggression needs to be brought out of the darkness into relational connectedness.

Many parents shy away from this because they feel uncomfortable. How do you talk about something so negative and destructive? Isn't it better to simply encourage the positive?

No, it's not. Your teen needs for all parts of himself—both the good and the bad—to be connected to you and others. He needs to experience his whole self in relationship with you, because that is what helps him to integrate and mature inside.

So take the plunge. Say, "I want to know what it was like when you got so mad at me that you threatened me. I will not tolerate this from you again, but I do want to listen to your side of it. Were you frustrated? Did you think I didn't understand? Did you think you had no other option?"

Bring your own experience into the relationship as well. Say, "It scared me when you got so angry at me. I felt cut off from you, like you were a stranger to me. I don't like feeling that way, so I want us to work on solving this." Your adolescent needs to be aware that his aggression affects others in significant ways.

Help your teen articulate negative feelings. Some aggressive teens have difficulty putting frustration and anger into words, and thus they act out violently. Like young children, they don't know how to symbolize feelings, so those feelings come out in actions.

You may need to help your teen develop a vocabulary regarding feelings. Talk to her about saying, "I am mad/sad/frustrated/ashamed/ scared." Tell her when you are feeling these emotions, and suggest them to her when she is upset. When teens see their parents appropriately articulating a range of emotions, they feel more secure in managing their own emotions and in expressing them as words.

Bring in resources. If your actions don't bring about more relatedness and self-control, you may need to bring in other resources to help. Groups and counselors can be a big help here.

Also, do not rescue your teen from the consequences of his anger. Your school probably has a protocol for aggression, involving detention, suspension, and even expulsion. Don't automatically assume these are bad for your teen. I have seen positive behavior change in teens whose parents have supported a school's efforts in this area.

If your teen's aggression is dangerous to others or himself, he may need to be placed in a residential treatment center or a boarding school that handles aggressive teens. Don't be afraid to send your child away. A treatment center may save his life.

You Can Do It!

Be the healthily aggressive antidote to your teen's unhealthy aggression. Take the initiative to help your kid become a balanced and integrated person who can control her behavior, be relational, and also solve her problems.

CHAPTER 22

Alcohol, Drugs, and Dependencies

It is every parent's nightmare: having a teen on drugs. This is not life as God designed it. Substance abuse causes the breakdown of all that is good. Enslavement replaces freedom. Detachment replaces love. Chaos replaces order. Despair replaces hope.

Many teens abuse alcohol and drugs, and this problem is not likely to go away anytime soon. I can't overstate the danger of substance abuse. It can, and often does, lead to poverty, injury, disease, and death.

But despite the seriousness of this problem, parents of teens with this issue need to understand that *the greatest single force to help a teen resolve a substance problem is an involved parent*. This chapter will give you guidelines for the process.

Defining the Problem

Unfortunately, the teen years are a perfect fit, in a sick way, for substance abuse problems. By nature, adolescents challenge the authority and values of parents and are highly susceptible to peer approval. They are interested in feelings and experiences, often to the neglect of good judgment, yet they can quickly become disconnected and can feel isolation deeply. Teens get easily bruised, discouraged, and hurt, and they gravitate toward quick ways to medicate the pain. No wonder the issue has become so far-reaching, particularly now that drugs are so accessible.

And they are accessible. Your teen likely knows how to get drugs if he wants them. He knows someone, or knows someone who knows someone. Be wise. Keep your head out of the sand and assume your teen has access.

If you accept this reality, it can assist you in helping your teen stay away from alcohol and drugs or in helping him recover from them.

Handling the Problem

You can't control whether your teen has access to drugs and alcohol, but you can support him and help him develop the internal restraints and strength he needs to resist using substances. Here are some ways to do just that.

Establish a zero tolerance policy. Be clear with your teen that substances are not acceptable and that you will not tolerate them. Your adolescent may be hearing muddy messages from lots of other sources, including friends and some of their parents. This is a black-and-white issue, not a gray one, so be direct about your stance on alcohol and drugs.

Not only should you be forthright about your stance, but also about the consequences. Let your adolescent know ahead of time that if she uses drugs or alcohol, she will lose many valued privileges and freedoms. Not only that, but if your teen continues to use, she will have to live somewhere else, because you have a value that substance abuse will not be tolerated in your home.

I know parents who have sent their teens to a different high school to get away from drug-using friends. I know some who have sent their kids to boarding schools. Others have sent their kids to residential treatment centers. And still others have done everything they could until the teen reached majority age, and then they made her move out of the house. Many times, this was absolutely the right move to make.

Such consequences may sound harsh, but only to those who are not experienced in the power and severity of drug problems. Substances are stronger than many people think, and their hold gets worse over time.

Come down hard at the first offense. If it is your teen's first offense, resist the impulse to say, "Oh well, first time, just don't do it again." *You will have only one first offense to deal with, and it is an opportunity to let your teen know that drugs and alcohol are not a casual deal.* Otherwise, your teen may think it's acceptable for him to use now and then.

Here are some suggestions for consequences:

Grounding. Grounding is a natural consequence, as your teen has shown that she can't resist temptation with her friends, so she can't have social contact with them for a significant period of time.

Supervised social contact. Allow your teen to go to social outings, including movies and parties, but only with an approved parent present. If he does not use substances during this period, he can then have more social freedom.

Drug testing. Home drug tests are now readily available. You can tell your teen that for the next few months you will be testing her randomly. A side benefit is that this also gives your teen an excuse not to use with friends. She can say, "I can't smoke pot. My parents do random testing."

Legal education. Some counties offer training for families in which they take teens through the court system as if they were going to jail, so that they can experience what the system would be like were they to be arrested and tried on a drug charge.

Service. Have your teen help out at the local rescue mission or church, doing errands, stocking the warehouse, or cleaning up. Learning the value of service often helps adolescents become open to the needs of others and can help break the self-absorption of substance use.

Live in the light. Our natural inclination as parents is to give our kids the information on the dangers of drugs and then hope they make good choices. But this is not enough. While your teen needs the information, she also needs *you*. She is not likely to say, "Would you ask me if I'm on drugs or not?" So be the parent and ask. Teens often hope on some level that their parents will ask, because they are scared and want to talk, but they are not about to ask a *parent*. Take the initiative to bring out drug matters into the light of relationship.

Listen when your teen talks. Try to get to the heart of what she understands, experiences, does, and feels. If you can't be shocked, you will be more likely to get more information. Your teen needs your viewpoint, but she also needs your ears.

Sometimes parents avoid talking about alcohol and drugs beyond the basic "don't do it" lecture. They think they might convey approval to the teen if they act interested in what is going on with friends and at school. Nothing could be further from the truth. Your teen is living in a drug-influenced world, whether or not she is using them. Don't leave her alone in that world. Enter it, be curious about it, and get to know it. Find out what kids are using and where, which parents are lax about substances, and where the parties are. Your involvement doesn't mean that you approve of drugs. It simply means you love your kid enough to get into her world.

Of course, being connected means more than talking about drugs. It involves being in an ongoing relationship with your teen about all aspects of her life. The more you connect on all levels, the more likely your teen will talk with you about any substance problem.

Know your teen. The better you know your adolescent, the better you will know how to respond to substance problems. Get to know what vulnerabilities are particular to your teen that drugs and alcohol might exploit, and get your teen the support, assistance, and structure he needs so that he is not so susceptible.

Here are some common vulnerabilities and ways you can deal with them.

She challenges your parenting and values. Find ways to have her safely question you that don't involve substances. Give her room and space to not be your clone.

He surrenders judgment to feelings and experiences. Spend time talking with him about that. Validate his need for experience, but help him develop the ability to make sound decisions, to think about the effects of his actions, and to postpone gratification for a greater good.

She is easily influenced by the approval of peers. Strengthen her individuality and character. Help her to say no to others, including you. Find healthy peers who will support her in this effort.

He is vulnerable to others. Have him make you the bad guy until he is stronger. For example, your teen may not be able to say, "No, I don't do drugs," but he can say, "My parents are really strict, and they would come down so hard on me if I did that." Not only is this statement true, but it gives your kid an out until he is firmer in his own values.

She disconnects and isolates quickly. Take initiative and draw her out. Be a bridge between your teen and her feelings, between herself and the world. Help her reconnect so that she doesn't need substances to feel alive.

He is easily hurt and is vulnerable to attempts to cover up his pain. Comfort and support your teen so that he can connect his hurt feelings to you so that they are less intense. At the same time, help him learn to confront and be honest with others so that he is stronger inside and less vulnerable.

Remember, now more than ever, your teen needs you to know who he is. Find out what he needs, what hurts him, and what matters to him. He may resist you, but part of him wants his parent to break through at some level so that he is not alone with himself.

Remember the druggies. In all likelihood, you were around drugs or at least had friends who were druggies when you were a teenager. Remember what potential they had? Some were smart, funny, creative, and gifted. Now think about where many of those people are today. Is that what you want for your teen's future? If your child's present is substance-influenced, it can easily become a substance-dominated future.

Seek help. If your teen is using alcohol or drugs, seek help. This complex problem requires much expertise, skill, and training. Fortunately, there are good counselors and teen workers who are well trained in substance problems. A good adolescent therapist can evaluate the severity of the problem and determine what structures will help the teen, ranging from counseling to an intensive detox and rehab program.

If your teen's drug and alcohol usage has moved beyond experimentation and become a regular part of her life, she now has a *dependency*. She now uses substances compulsively, no matter how negative the life consequences have become. She cannot stop on her own and will need outside support and expertise.

Watch out for other types of dependency. Dependencies are not limited to drugs and alcohol. A teen can become a sex addict, for example, from viewing pornographic websites, and be trapped in compulsive behaviors that keep him returning to the sexual images. These teens feel intense shame, guilt, and helplessness about their porn addictions. Youth pastors and counselors can do much to help kids deal with this issue.

In addition, some teens also have food dependencies known as eating disorders, such as anorexia, bulimia, and obesity. In such instances, eating habits and food intake become the focus of life, sometimes to the point of being life-threatening. Teens with these dependencies can make good progress in resolving them when they receive competent help.

You Can Do It!

Be proactive, informed, and involved. The sooner you deal with your teen's abuse of alcohol, drugs, sex, or food, the more likely your teen will get back on the road to a healthy life. Your involvement can save your child's life.

CHAPTER 23

Argumentativeness

The phrase "argumentative teen" seems redundant. Adolescents often have the verbal ability of an adult, and they also have the energy to push an issue to infinite lengths.

Sometimes they argue to be provocative and get a reaction from you. More often, they argue as a way of resisting a limit you have imposed. They will give many, many reasons why you're wrong about your position on a curfew, a behavior problem, or a school problem. Sometimes their reasons even contradict each other, as in the following example:

Teen: "No other parents are making their daughters dress like this for the dance."

Parent: "Well, I think appropriate clothing is important. I'm sorry you feel like you're the only one who is being singled out."

Teen: "Well, I am."

Parent: "I've talked to several other parents who feel the same way we do about how girls are dressing. I've found there are lots of us."

Teen: "Well, why do you guys have to do what everybody else does?"

Welcome to the teen argument. Just remember that for them, the goal isn't the truth; it's freedom.

Even so, as the parent you need to listen to your teen's point of view. Kids need their parents to hear what they have to say; and besides, you could be wrong.

Just today I changed my mind because of a kid's feedback. One of my sons wanted to go to the park to hang out with his friends for an hour, and I had some chores for him to do afterward. For some unthinking reason, I gave him a hard time about coming home on time, saying, "Remember, you're going to have a consequence if you're back late."

"Whoa," he said. "Why are you getting all over me? I'm pretty good about that."

He was right; he was seldom late. "Sorry about that," I said.

So listen and understand. But at the same time, be the parent. You have the final say.

Defining the Problem

Home is where adolescents forge their ability to question, think for themselves, and take responsibility for their lives, and healthy arguing is a part of that process. Arguing can help them develop an *increased sense of ownership over their lives.*

If your teen is sincerely open about a matter and isn't challenging you simply to get her way, don't shut her down. Instead, encourage her. For example, if she questions your prohibition on underage drinking, say, "Are you willing to see my side of it if I will see your side?" Help her see that the issue is about truth, health, maturity, and morality rather than what she wants.

But if you notice that arguments are a constant, that your teen argues about every issue and problem, and that she is relentless, then you may need to address the argumentativeness itself as a problem.

Handling the Problem

Bring the problem into the relationship. Have a talk, not about the topic your teen is arguing about, but about the argumentativeness. Help him be aware that it exists, and let him know how it affects people by telling him something like this: "You seem to argue with me over lots and lots of things, and it doesn't seem to ever get better. I think I am trying to see your point of view, and if I'm not, tell me. But I don't see that you are seeing my point of view, and that doesn't work for me. I want you to be aware of this and not have to win every disagreement we have. I want you to have freedom, but when you are so disagreeable, it tells me that you might not be ready for it yet."

In addition to talking about the argumentativeness, it sometimes helps when parents detach from the fight and observe the pattern of their teen's behavior. For example, let's say you're having a battle over the car. Your teen demands to use it to go out, but you drive the car to work. He won't take no for an answer and gets louder and angrier.

At that point, stop using reason and logic. Wait until your teen draws a breath, then say, "This is what I was talking about. Do you see it?"

"I don't see anything but how selfish you are!"

"I know, but look at what's going on. This happens all the time. I want you to be aware of how you get so argumentative and angry, whether the argument is about a big deal or a little deal."

"Well, if you wouldn't — "

"I'm not talking about that. I hope you are listening, because I'm going to keep bringing this up so that you can see that arguing is a pattern for you. I want you to start learning to discuss differences without getting so angry, and I'm going to insist on this."

Such observations help your teen become more and more aware, though he may initially refuse to see that he can't disagree without fighting. Awareness of a problem is the first step toward change.

Be patient, but set a limit. Though you want to hear your teen out, when you realize that the issue isn't about right and wrong, fair and unfair, but about trying to get you to change your mind, put a limit on how far the conversation goes. Parents who don't do this are training teens to think that people will give them all the time in the world to wear them down. Not good preparation for becoming a successful adult.

So be patient and hear your teen out, but set a limit. At some point, you may need to say something like this: "Luci, I think I understand your thinking about your dress. You think that all of my suggestions for something more modest are going to be embarrassing ones for you. And you think that the dress I don't want is fine and that I am overreacting.

The negotiation and compromise haven't worked this time. So I will have to say no."

If Luci continues with another reason, you may want to say, "I think I've heard all the reasons and thoughts you have. So I'm ending this conversation now. Maybe we can return to it later, but for now, I want to talk about something else."

"But you're being so unfair!"

"I'm sorry you feel that way. I'm going to make a sandwich; want one?"

"You are so mean!"

"I'm thinking you're becoming disrespectful now. So I'm going to leave your room and give you a little time for yourself. If you continue this conversation at this point, there will be a consequence."

Remember, it's not your job to get your teen to agree or to be happy with you. Your job is to love her and help her live within the parameters of reasonable realities. All of us, teens included, have to submit to authority at times, whether it be a boss, a highway patrolman, or the IRS. So when you've been patient and understanding for a reasonable length of time, and your teen still keeps arguing, assert your authority and say, "I love you, but this conversation is over for now."

Still, the authority card is not one you want to play often. If you find yourself needing to do so, then your teen might have a respect problem. If so, you might want to show her more love and consistency so that your words are heeded more.

Establish and enforce the consequence. Suppose, however, you have done all the above, and your teen insists on arguing to the point of distraction. It may be time to set a limit.

You might approach it this way: "I want to know how you feel when you think I'm wrong about a limit, and I will listen to what you say. But right now it seems you simply want to talk me out of a lot of decisions I am making. So I will listen to you, to a point, and I will give you my reasons for my decision, to a point. But if you insist on arguing with me after we've done that a few times, I will double whatever limit we are discussing. So if you are arguing about having to come home an hour earlier than you would like, you will have to come in two hours earlier. I really want you to get hold of your behavior."

As always, be sure to follow through. Argumentative teens almost always need to experience consequences, as they are often used to a parent who gives in and gives up. So talk with your teen, set the limit, and then keep it.

You Can Do It!

Keep the future in mind. You want your teen to become an adult who can challenge and confront others. But you also want him to know when it's time to fold his cards and accept the way things are. That is the way of wisdom.

CHAPTER 24

Breaking Agreements

'll return Nicole's phone."

"I'll mow the lawn tomorrow."

"I'll pay you back next week."

"I'll get my homework done this weekend."

"I'll be at the parking lot at 3:00 p.m. for the car pool."

Adolescents, like all of us, make many different kinds of agreements.

Agreements and promises are important parts of life. Love, friendships, and even business are built on them. They undergird and support trusting, dependable, and safe relationships. When people stand by their words, life goes better. When they do not, life often comes apart at some level. While no one follows through perfectly, if your teen has a habit of making promises that he doesn't fulfill, it affects him, you, the family, and your teen's relationships.

Defining the Problem

Many teens do not have the capacity to keep agreements. To do so requires good judgment, a basis in reality, an orientation toward the future, and an understanding of what is being agreed to. Few adolescents have honed these skills. So they make all sorts of promises without thinking about what is involved. Their thought process is similar to that of a credit card addict who is eternally optimistic: *I'll pay off the debt later.* But later never comes, and the debt continues to mount.

If your teen isn't good at keeping commitments, have some compassion while you work with her on this. It is less likely to be about defiance and deception than about having limited experience and judgment in this part of life. Of course, some teens do make agreements with no intention of keeping them, and that is a matter of deception (see chapter 29, "Deception and Lying"), but most aren't that way.

As your teen learns to make and keep agreements, she is also developing a future orientation, which will be invaluable. The capacity to ask, *How will what I am doing now affect my future?* will assist her in impulse control, delay of gratification, frustration tolerance, and goal achievement. Your adolescent's ability to keep her agreements affects a broad range of her life, today and tomorrow.

Keeping agreements is not the same as following house rules and requirements. Those are formal, often written, and are broad expectations of chores, behavior, and attitude. Agreements are more informal and have to do with situations that just come up and that require a quick negotiation. You can't have a rule about every agreement in life. That would require a giant notebook. But as we shall see, *you can have an expectation about making agreements.*

Handling the Problem

Here are some ways to help your teen put his "saying" and his "doing" together.

Get the problem out in the open. First, talk and bring the issue into the relationship. Be warm and accepting, but also be direct. Approach the issue as a problem to be solved by both of you: "Stacy, I've noticed that you make a lot of promises, but that you have trouble keeping up your end. For example, last week when you said you would sort out your clothes to give to charity, it never happened. And yesterday, you said you would fill the car with gas, and it's empty today."

"I was busy. You know how much homework I had."

"I know you have a lot of homework. But when you agree to do something, it affects other people, and we depend on you. When you don't follow through, it makes things difficult, and I have a harder time trusting you. That is a problem, and I want us to work on it."

This first step will often cause your teen to be somewhat more aware that breaking agreements is an issue. It usually doesn't solve the problem, but making her aware of a pattern you are observing can help.

Give your teen a way to think before making an agreement. Again, most adolescents don't understand how to think about agreements, especially if they have never been required to keep them. Here's an example of a conversation you might have to help your teen learn to think through an agreement.

You might begin by saying, "I think that sometimes you will agree to do something to get me off your back and stop bugging you. Or sometimes it's because you think you can get to it at the time. I understand that. But I want to help you start thinking through this more."

"Like what?"

"Well, maybe you should have told me you didn't have time to sort your clothes because of finals. I would have understood, and we could have scheduled it for a better time."

"You get mad when I say I don't have time to do something."

"Yes, I have done that. But if it's reasonable, I want to listen to you better. But sometimes it has nothing to do with me; you simply don't think about whether you have the time to do what I ask. You're a little overly optimistic about what you think you can do. Do you think this is possible?"

"Maybe."

"Well, most people can do that. I certainly have. But before you say you will do something, it's important to think through whether you can and will do what you say. I would rather you say you can't than have you say one thing and do another. Would it help if, next time, I reminded you to think about it before you make a promise to me?"

By having a conversation like this, you are helping to make your teen more aware when he is making an agreement, and that others are negatively affected if he breaks it. And you make yourself available to remind him to think the agreement through until he starts thinking about it on his own.

Establish consequences. Even so, awareness and guidance may not be enough to help your teen think before making an agreement. If this proves to be so, then you may need to provide the structure that consequences bring.

Don't drive yourself and your teen crazy with specific consequences for each and every failed agreement. Make it about the bigger issue. Say, "It seems you're still not following up with what I have been asking you to do. So until you improve in this area, I'm going to take away your phone privileges for a couple of days. I'm not asking you to be perfect, but I want to see the pattern change."

Sometimes parents make it a consequence that the teen has to do what she said she would do, but this approach often doesn't solve the problem. The worst that can happen is that she has to do the task and has an annoyed parent. In the best scenario you will forget to ask her to do what she agreed to do, or she will have bought herself some time.

So require follow-up, but have a separate consequence. This helps your teen be more aware of how her inaction will affect her in ways that she would like to avoid.

You Can Do It!

Your teen needs you to help him become a person whose word means something, for then he will be happier, and his relationships will be better as well.

CHAPTER 25

Chores

My family was invited to a friend's home for dinner. When I walked into their home, the teens were watching television, and the mom was running around the kitchen, frantically doing everything.

I said to her, "Why aren't you getting the kids to help?"

"It's too much trouble."

"I don't know," I said. "What you are doing now looks like trouble to me."

Defining the Problem

Household chores are part of everyday life. While all kids can help out in some way, teenagers should be doing advanced chores, the kind that they will have to be doing when they move out. They need to learn to clean up after themselves, set and clear the table, load and unload the dishwasher (or wash the dishes), do laundry, work in the yard, and cook. Being in a family means taking part in family responsibilities that need getting done.

But there is a deeper, more important reason parents need to require their kids to do chores. Doing chores helps your teen be who she was created to be. Life, as designed by God, can most simply be described as two things: connecting and doing, or love and task. Everything we do that is meaningful is either about relationships, love, and connectedness, or about tasks, responsibilities, and work.

In fact, the first command given to the human race had to do with tasks: God blessed them and said, "Be fruitful and increase in number; fill the earth and subdue it."[25] We were designed to be fruitful and to take stewardship over the world. So when your teen does the dishes, she is taking part in God's grand design.

But that's not all. Life requires adults to fulfill many tasks: work and career responsibilities, household maintenance responsibilities, parenting responsibilities, finances, and the like. When parents require teens to do chores, they are helping prepare their teens to succeed in their future responsibilities. Far better for teens to have years of experience of doing certain chores, because they can then move smoothly into taking on the grown-up tasks of life.

Handling the Problem

Most of the time, when chores get neglected, it's as much the fault of the parent as it is the teen. Parents fall into a few common traps that result in nothing being done. Once you are aware of and resolve these traps, your job is much easier. When parents are the problem, it's typically for one of three reasons: they fail to provide clear structure, they give up because it feels like too much trouble, or they fail to insist on chores because of all the other demands on the teen's life.

Establish a clear structure. Of all the problems this book addresses, chores are probably the easiest to structure. Give your teen specific responsibilities to be done at a certain level of competence and with some regularity, and establish a consequence if they are not done. Simply say, "No phone or television until the kitchen is clean," or "No going out on the weekend until the yard is done." Such arrangements have meaning for teens; they see how what they want is dependent on what they do.

Many great charts are available for helping kids do their chores. I just searched online for "family chore charts" and found almost 45,000 websites on the topic!

But most of the time, instead of structuring house maintenance, parents tell their teen to clean up better after himself, and then they get annoyed when he doesn't, which is most of the time.

So if you haven't already, take the time to set up your expectations regarding chores, tailored to your own family. If you haven't taken this step, you are likely doing too many chores yourself. And don't reward kids for doing their household chores. You might reward a four-year-old the first time he cleans up his room. But a teen who expects a reward for doing what's expected will be set up for disappointment when he doesn't get regularly rewarded by a spouse for cleaning up.

Always require some chores. Your teen may have other legitimate demands on her life. Homework, sports, cultural activities, social outings, and church can take a lot of time. Some parents feel like they are already asking so much of their kids that it isn't fair to insist that they do chores. Others struggle because the teen isn't around when the chores need to be done. If the trash is to be taken out on Thursday night, and your teen has sports and studies until late on Thursdays, how can she help take out the trash?

These are realities, and there is no easy solution. If your teen is doing well in school and life, with a good attitude, and it takes all her time to accomplish her goals, you may need to require less of her. You certainly don't want to overwhelm her.

But do require something. Teens should help out by doing regular tasks at home. Chores are a very important developmental part of life. If there isn't time for chores, it may be a sign that your teen is too busy and needs your help in balancing his life. Sometimes the parent needs to step in and have the teen curtail some activities.

Enforce the chores. Following through with consequences takes work, but *the chore of the parent is to enforce the chore of the teen.* This can be a lot of effort and trouble, at least until doing chores becomes a habit in the teen's mind.

In many homes, the parent and teen engage in a waiting game when it comes to chores. If the teen can patiently protest, argue, sneak past, and defy, the parent may get worn down and give up. The sign that the parent is waving the white flag is the classic, "Never mind. It's easier for me to do it than to get you to do it!"

If you have said and done this, you are not alone. All parents do it. But take the hard road here. Do the difficult work of investing in your adolescent. If you can stay consistent with reasonable and fair consequences over time, you will outwait your teen, and things should become better. Never forget the goal: a young adult who knows how to be responsible, how to work, and how to take care of himself. You are preventing a blowout later in life.

Keep in mind that avoidance and defiance can also be part of the problem. There is a big, interesting world out there, and your teen's life is quickly moving in that direction, not toward home. You must always remember that the next time you feel abandoned by your teen because he didn't do an assigned chore. His neglect often is not about you but about your adolescent's immature efforts to join his world. He needs you to help him learn to fulfill his responsibilities before he runs out and joins the world!

So don't personalize your teen's chore avoidance and protest. Just lovingly and patiently stick with the consequences until it becomes more trouble for him to fight than to take out the garbage.

You Can Do It!

Chores, which sound boring and mundane, provide something very valuable for your teen: the gifts of self-control, diligence, faithfulness, and responsibility. Whichever of those 45,000 charts you pick, if it works for you, stick with it!

CHAPTER 26

Clothing

"There's nothing wrong with my blouse."

"Get off my back; the words on my T-shirt are my business."

"Everybody wears their jeans like this."

"You can't tell me what to wear."

Defining the Problem

Clothes, which are very important to teens, can be the cause of major arguments between parents and their kids. While on the surface this may seem a minor problem, clothes do matter because of what those clothes may be saying about the wearer.

Inappropriate clothing for adolescents includes clothes that are too revealing and sexual; clothes that contain advertisements for negative influences, such as drugs, sex, violence, and death; or clothes that reflect alliances with unhealthy cultures, such as gangs.

Handling the Problem

Here are some ways to deal with teen clothing issues.

Allow for individual style. Clothing plays an important role in the development of your teen. An adolescent is becoming a person in her own right and is working on differentiating from her parents. She needs space and a way to do this in a safe manner, and clothing style is one of the ways teens can indicate they are not like their parents, and are identifying with peers, as they prepare to form their own values, feelings, and attitudes. An adolescent's clothing reflects her inner differences with the parent.

In most cases, when teens feel more established in their identity, their clothing becomes less extreme. This is a sign that they have individuated and feel more secure and solid internally. They may even identify somewhat with things they like about their parents, because they no longer need to distinguish themselves. They may even wear dresses and slacks sometimes!

So don't react negatively to your teen's choice of attire, as you will then set up a power struggle that can make this period worse than it has to be. In addition, keep some perspective about this issue. Some of the most troubled kids I have worked with dressed very conservatively. On the other hand, I know some great kids who dress weird, but are doing well in relationships, family, and growth. How your teen is doing in these areas likely matters more than what clothes he wears.

Realize that clothes have meaning. Don't make the mistake of trying to get a kid to dress better without understanding her insides. Jesus told the hypocritically religious Pharisees that they were focusing on the externals to the neglect of the more important internals: "Blind Pharisee! First clean the inside of the cup and dish, and then the outside also will be clean."[26]

Clothing styles, especially unacceptable ones, have meaning. They can tell you a great deal about your teen's inner world: what is important to her, how she feels about herself, and what she thinks about her relationships. For example:

- Inappropriate styles may indicate a need for peer approval.
- Sexualized styles can be a sign that a girl depends more on her body than her character to attract boys.
- Dark themes, such as death, drugs, and violence, can indicate internal alienation, rage, or rebellion.
- Culturally based clothing, such as gang styles, may manifest inappropriate values.

If you can understand what your teen's clothes may be conveying, you can help her at a significant level, and you will likely see some positive changes in her style of clothing.

Character generally comes out in themes, so you should notice your teen's behavior patterns reflected in what she wears. This will help you to talk about what is going on underneath the clothes. For example, if you see alienation, say, "It's not just that you wear all black every day; it's that it seems you've withdrawn from people who care about you. I need for us to talk, because I don't know how you are doing inside." If you see sexual themes, say, "I know you want to be attractive to boys. There's nothing wrong with that. But it seems to me that you are willing to be what you think boys want you to be, and that may not be who you really are. Can we talk about that?" Stay with themes and don't leave it with the clothes.

So be wise, and look at your teen's clothing in the context of her character and what you know about her.

Don't moralize or overidentify. Most parents have two opposite reactions to teen clothing issues, and neither of them works. The first reaction is to interpret differences as scary and destructive. This can be a mistake, as these parents are *moralizing a preference*. Remember, if you don't like a particular style of clothing, the clothes aren't necessarily morally reprehensible. Clothing styles are usually a matter of preference, not morality.

The other reaction is *overidentification*. Parents overidentify when, in an attempt to connect, they adopt the dress of the adolescent. However, this often backfires. While the intent may be good, this overidentification forces the teen to differentiate even further, in the service of individuating from the parent. So a dad who wants to look like a punker for his kid will often find that the kid will then try to find an extreme style that will help him to be different from his dad.

Kids need a generation gap so they can figure out who they are. You can learn to connect without looking like a teen. Be a grown-up. Your teen needs to be around an adult.

Deal with the inappropriate. However, having said all that, you still should confront your adolescent's inappropriate attire. You want your teen to be responsible for what he wears and how it affects others.

Begin by working out an agreement of definitions of inappropriateness, such as:

- clothing that draws too much attention to the body and distracts from the face and character;
- words and graphics that convey dark themes;
- styles that are so bizarre that they interfere with school and relationships; and
- clothes that say something about the teen that isn't who the teen really is.

Get lots of input from your teen here so that he is involved and has choices. The more he buys into the definitions, the less he will argue later.

Give your teen as much freedom as possible in this area. Whatever does not cross the established lines is okay. If your teen disagrees with the lines, and you have tried to involve him and be reasonable, say, "Until you can work with me on this, these are the standards and requirements. I want you to have as much latitude as is reasonable, but for now, these are the clothing rules."

If your kid continues to cross the established lines regarding dress, you should impose a consequence and say something like this: "If you insist on dressing these ways, you will lose whatever social setting you want to wear them in." That means the people she is dressing for won't see the clothing. This consequence helps take some motivation out of the improper dress.

Refrain from getting into power struggles. If your teen is leaving for school dressed inappropriately, ask her only once to change the clothes. Don't try to force her to do so if she refuses. If she refuses, remind her of the consequence and let her choice determine her social future.

You Can Do It!

Save your energy for more important issues than clothes. But be aware of what clothing says about your teen's heart and feelings. They are a window to your child's inner self.

CHAPTER 27

Curfew Violations

It's Friday night, and your teenage son is having some chill time with his buddies at a friend's home. They are listening to music, playing video games, watching television, eating, and joking around. After a hard week at school, your son is really kicking back.

He glances at his watch and realizes he has about five minutes to leave in order to get home on time. But right then, one of his friends tells him it's his turn to compete in the video competition, and he is pretty good at this particular game.

Your son doesn't think, *I am choosing to get home late.* Adolescents don't think like that. He thinks, *I can do this game pretty fast.* But of course, reality wins over his wishful thinking, and he misses his curfew.

Defining the Problem

Curfew problems are underrated. Most parents miss the real value of setting good curfew limits and boundaries. *Adolescents need to learn how to disengage from what they love in order to meet their responsibilities.* That is such a helpful skill in adult life.

Imagine the career future of a young adult who can leave some conversation or project, budget enough time to get to the next meeting, and arrive on time and ready. This is the stuff that CEOs are built of.

And curfews can help teens in the world of relationships too. A person who is dependable, faithful, and focused is a person who attracts and takes care of good and healthy relationships. So don't underestimate the power of curfew boundaries.

Handling the Problem

If you want to keep curfew problems to a minimum, here are some things you can do.

Make sure your curfew is reasonable. As your teen gets increasingly engaged in the world outside your sphere, she will most likely need a curfew. Having to be home by an established time will protect her time and life and help her learn responsibility. A curfew will also enable your family to keep some order.

Before your teen heads out for the evening, be clear about her curfew and the consequence for violating it. For instance, you might say, "Have a great time. I expect you home by 10:00 p.m. If you choose to be late, you won't be able to go out the next time you want to hang out with your friends."

Keep in mind the characteristics of a good curfew.

A good curfew allows enough time for relationship. The curfew needs to be late enough so that your teen has a few hours to do something meaningful with friends. If it is too strict and early, he can't connect with his new world at a level where he can be attached. A teen's relational cup needs time in order to get filled.

But if your teen is the last of her friends to go home, because all the other kids have earlier curfews, she is no longer in community. This defeats the purpose of relationship. Get with parents you think are sound, and if possible, agree on a time for all the kids.

A good curfew provides for safety. Make the curfew early enough to protect your teen from being in situations where he might be vulnerable. This, of course, depends on your kid's age and maturity level. For example, a fourteen-year-old who hangs out at the mall should probably not be out in the parking lot after the mall closes. Also be aware of your local area's curfew laws, especially concerning teens who are driving.

A good curfew allows for sufficient sleep time. Make sure the curfew takes into account how much sleep your teen needs. Take into consideration when she has to get up and what she has to do the next day. Protect her tomorrow for her.

A good curfew has the teen's buy in. As much as possible, involve your teen in curfew setting. Curfews should change with the teen's increasing age and maturity. Listen to his end of things, and use his input.

When kids miss their curfew, parents can worry because they don't know if the kid is okay. How can you know when to stay up and when to go to bed?

Know when to wait up. This depends on the teen. If he has an on-time history and isn't sneaky or deceptive, you are probably safe in going to bed. But if your teen has problems keeping curfew, or if he has sneaked in and out of the house, stay up. He needs more structure and presence from you until he is more aware and responsible in this area.

Whether you wait up or not, you'll need to deal with the missed curfew.

Deal with violations. Here are some straightforward guidelines for what to do if your teen violates curfew.

Establish a consequence and follow through with it. Remember how consequences work; they are the addition of something the teen doesn't want or the removal of something she does want. They are meant to affect your teen's future more than they are meant to be preventative. So when teens violate their curfew, it makes sense to take away some social time.

But don't just tell your teen the consequence. If she is late, follow through. You are helping her to create the ability to disengage from what she is doing in order to be responsible for a future obligation.

Differentiate between reasons and excuses. Sometimes parents have difficulty telling the difference between a valid reason and an excuse. It helps to think out these matters ahead of time, and with your teen. Though you won't anticipate everything, you should have fewer arguments.

Here are some typical things kids say to justify why they missed curfew, along with my responses.

"I had an emergency!" Certainly medical emergencies and car problems are legitimate reasons for missing curfew. Just reserve the

word *emergency* for the real thing. For example, running out of gas is not an emergency, because the teen could have prevented that from happening.

"My ride was late." A reason the first time, but if your teen says this often, something else is going on. He may need to experience the consequence so that he will structure his friend's time or get another ride.

"I lost track of time." Always an excuse, never a reason. Being away from home is a privilege.

"The movie got out late." An excuse, not a reason. Movie times are published. Your teen can plan for this issue before going out.

"But I called to tell you I would be late." While it's good that your teen was thoughtful enough to call, that doesn't change the fact that she violated her curfew.

You Can Do It!

Unlike some of the other behavior problems, teens who violate curfew are motivated to change when the problem behavior results in their not being able to spend time with friends. In most cases, you will see positive changes if you establish reasonable limits and follow through on them, and you will help your teen learn to deal better with time and responsibility. So let your creaky floor stay creaky, and pay attention to when your kid comes home.

CHAPTER 28

Cutting and Self-Mutilation

Gayle had recently found out that her son Dennis was a "cutter"; that is, he was in the habit of making small, shallow incisions on his arms with a pocketknife. She was understandably concerned and frightened about this.

When I asked her how she found out Dennis was self-mutilating, she said, "That's the funny part. He's quiet anyway, so I didn't have any suspicions. What finally tipped me off was the long-sleeved shirts in hot weather. If not for that, I don't know how long it would have been before I found out."

Defining the Problem

Cutting and other forms of self-mutilation have been around for a while, but they are becoming more popular with teens. The habit crosses all socioeconomic lines; poor kids and rich kids are doing it. Cutting is at best disturbing and at worst very dangerous to your adolescent.

There are various types of self-mutilation as well as varying levels of severity, but cutting and burning are the most common. Some kids, like Dennis, will use knives, razors, pens, or pencils to periodically cut themselves on the arms, legs, or other parts of the body, leaving long, shallow scratches. Sometimes they cut deeply enough to scar, but not always. In severe cases, a teen will cut himself deeply enough to bleed at dangerous levels, and there is always the risk of infection. I even dealt with a severe case in which the teen cut off his finger.

Other kids will burn themselves with cigarettes or lighters, leaving small round marks. Often they will pick at the scabs, which can cause infections. Some teens will strike themselves or bang their heads on the wall. While tattooing and skin piercing are sometimes considered self-mutilation, they are more about style, which is very different from cutting and burning.

Sometimes teens will expose their cuts or burns by wearing clothes that reveal them. This can point to a desire for a parent or peer to notice that they are having a problem without having to verbalize the problem. It is a cry for help.

Self-mutilation almost always indicates the presence of a deeper issue, even though your teen may have no idea what that issue is. A good deal of research has gone into finding out why an adolescent would do something to himself that seems so sick and destructive. Most of the time, the habit has more to do with something inside that is hurting the teen.

Here are some common reasons kids cut or self-mutilate.

They feel nothing, and pain makes them feel alive. When a teen is disconnected from his own emotions, as well as from other people, he often feels unreal, as if he doesn't exist. Because our emotions give us the sense that we are alive, an emotionally disconnected teen may engage in cutting in order to feel something. Pain is better than being numb.

They need a way to outwardly express inner pain. Some teens carry enormous amounts of emotional hurt inside, including grief, guilt, anger, and fear, which they are often unable to articulate. Self-mutilation gives them an outward way to identify with their inner pain. Sometimes a teen will tell me, "My outsides match my insides when I cut."

They feel they deserve to be punished. If an adolescent feels he is a bad person or has done things that he should be punished for, he may hurt his body in a symbolic attempt to receive the punishment. He acts as if he is criminal, judge, and jury.

They are reenacting some abuse or trauma to try and resolve it. Kids who have suffered from abuse or trauma will sometimes cut or burn. They may be reliving or reenacting the traumatic experience in order to work through it and resolve it. Of course, cutting or burning doesn't help them resolve the trauma, so they keep trying and self-mutilating.

They want to replace bad feelings with good feelings. Some researchers think that the pain of self-mutilation releases endorphins, substances in the body that create a sense of well-being, as if you have just had a good workout. They believe that some teens self-mutilate because they are looking for a good feeling to medicate bad ones, in a self-soothing manner.

They want to connect with peers. Some teens do not yet have a secure and stable sense of self. They lack a cohesive identity. As a result, they see the cutting and burning as yet another cool thing that may help them connect with others. They are identifying with adolescents who are in rebellion against parents, teachers, and other authorities.

They may have a biochemical issue. In some cases the reason for cutting is physiologically induced rather than emotionally. The teen may have a chemical imbalance and may need medical attention in order to treat the condition.

Handling the Problem

If your teen is self-mutilating, don't pass it off as an adolescent phase, but don't panic either. Your teen needs your understanding and your action. Here are some guidelines for what to do if your teen is cutting or burning.

Talk with your teen and try to figure out any patterns. Sit down and say, "I know you are cutting yourself. I am trying to learn about this so I can help you, and I am not mad at you. But I am serious that we will deal with this. So I want you to tell me everything you know about when you do it, how often, for how long, with whom, and why, as far as you know."

Don't settle for the inevitable "I don't know." Insist that she talk about what might trigger it: for instance, loss, failure, a boyfriend/

girlfriend problem, school stress, or a family problem. As much as you can, figure out the patterns, because you'll likely find something meaningful in them.

Help your teen identify the underlying problem. If you find a clear pattern, help your teen understand the underlying problem. For example, you might say something like this: "I think I understand that you cut yourself when you are mad at me or feeling lonely or scared. Is that right?"

If the teen agrees, say, "I want to help you with this. Cutting is not okay, it's not good for you, and it can be dangerous." Ask if there is something you're doing that keeps your teen from entrusting her problems to you. Work on your relationship and on openness. Help her work on the underlying problem, and tell her you will be checking on her to see if the cutting continues.

If the behavior continues, consult a therapist, for you don't want to let it go on. Most adolescent specialists are trained to understand and intervene with self-mutiliation, and an experienced one can help your teen resolve the issue.

You Can Do It!

Most of all, be an involved parent. Face the problem, insist on bringing it into your relationship by talking about it and working on it together, and seek help if the behavior continues. While this problem can be frightening, it can also be dealt with successfully.

CHAPTER 29

Deception and Lying

It's Sunday night and your son wants to play video games. You remind him that the rule is that he has to finish all his homework before he can have fun, but he insists that he doesn't have any homework. You take him at his word, then later you find out that he had a test the next Monday and got a failing grade on it.

Your son didn't yell, "You can't make me do homework!" Instead, he sneaked around you.

Defining the Problem

When your teen deceives you, she is hiding herself from you, and *you don't know her.* Your teen is not present with you. And that is not good. If your adolescent is lying, you need to first understand why. Let's explore three common reasons.

Fear. Sometimes a teen is deceptive because he is afraid to be honest. He may be scared that he will disappoint you or a friend. He may be afraid of being direct about his differences with you, or he may be afraid of your anger or that you will pull away from him.

The cause of a teen's deception is often rooted in a conflict between truth and relationship. At some level, *your teen may fear that the truth*

187

will interfere with love. He fears that the truth will not result in relationship but instead damage or destroy the relationship.

If this is the situation with your teen, help him feel safe about relationship. Ask if you are not letting your teen be real, or if you are controlling his life so much that he has no freedom or secrets. Let him know that you may not agree with or like things he says, but that no matter what, you are on his side. Reassure your teen that you will love him no matter what he says or does, and encourage him to take a risk with you to see if this is true. Tell him you want him to have love, space, and freedom. In doing these things, you are helping your teen to integrate truth with love, which is something he deeply needs.

Parental double binds. Sometimes a parent will inadvertently put the adolescent in a no-win situation in which the kid is almost forced to lie. That is, the parent makes a rule that is not realistic, and the teen can't win.

Here's an example. I told my son that he couldn't hang around with Steven, whom I thought was a bad influence. Steven was out of control and into drinking and drugs. My son liked Steven, and I was concerned that he was vulnerable to him. My son agreed to do what I asked. Not long after that, a group of my son's friends got together, and Steven was among them. My son felt weird and embarrassed about walking away from the group, so he didn't do anything about it, nor did he tell me about it.

I found out about it, and when I talked with him about what had happened, I realized that I had put my son in a bad situation. I thought about it, and I told him that while I wished he had told me about it himself, I realized that it was a better idea for him to agree to not being alone with Steven. In a group, my kid was not really vulnerable to Steven. The real danger was when they were alone.

Your kid's life is challenging enough. She doesn't need you to make unnecessary rules and demands on her.

A shortcut mentality. Sometimes teens lie because lying is easier than telling the truth; they have an internal conflict about deception. To them, lying seems more practical. While all of us have this shortcut mentality at some level, you don't want your teen to develop a pattern of chronic lying and deception, which can ruin a person's life.

It's one thing to understand why your teen resorts to deception and lies; it's another to help her change.

Handling the Problem

Remember the lies you told during this period of your life. Have some compassion as you sort through this issue with your teen. In addition, here are some ways you can help your teen become more direct and honest.

Take a no-tolerance stand. To address this problem, you need to take a clear and direct stance that you will not tolerate deception. Let your teen know that you will have zero tolerance toward deception and that there is no such thing as a white lie. Deception is deception.

I don't mean to sound too harsh here. Handle this problem, like all problems with your teen, with love, acceptance, and grace. But allow your teen to experience the reality that it is not okay, and will never be okay, for him to fudge on where he was and whom he was with. By taking a firm stance on this problem, you can help your teen develop a character that values truth as well as relationship. He needs to understand that *when deception begins, relationship ends.*

Stay connected, even in the problem. This is very important. Remember that this is your teen's dark side, and she needs to know that you know it and that you will keep her dark side in the relationship. At the same time, let her know how her lying makes the connection difficult. Appeal to your relationship. For example, you might say, "I am always for you, regardless of whether you lie. But when you deceive me, it is hard to know who you are or to believe you. I want a relationship with you, and I am going to keep working on this with you. But I want you to know that deception gets in the way of that." Your teen needs to hear that when she's dishonest she is distancing herself from the relationship.

Make it clear that love is free, but that freedom is earned. Remember the foundational principle that teens want freedom—and lots of it! Let your teen know that *to the extent that he is untruthful, he loses the freedom he desires.* He needs to understand that while your love for him is unconditional and freely given, you have to trust him to give him more rope, so he chooses how much freedom he has. Tell him, "I know you want to go out more. But your lying makes it impossible for me to trust you. So you will be going out less often until I see more honesty in you."

Give your teen a way to earn freedom. Once you have taken the steps outlined above, give your teen a little freedom and see what she does with it. For example, you might say that she can go out with her friends but that for now, because of the lying, she has to call you several times while she's out and that an adult has to get on the line to verify that she is where she said she was going to be.

This requires a lot of work on your part, and it will take some doing. She will say that she can't always be with adults. But she needs to know that deception is serious and that the way for her to get more freedom is by slowly gaining back your trust.

Go lighter on confession, heavier on deception. Let your adolescent know that if he breaks a rule, it will go better for him if he admits the truth rather than being caught in a lie. If he has been deceptive, the consequence will be much higher than if he had simply confessed the transgression to you.

Catch what you can, but stay focused on the relationship. At the same time, don't expect to know everything and catch everything. Don't cause your kid to think you are going to monitor every second of her life. That often makes kids more creatively deceptive. A teen who is lying, and intends to lie, will inevitably get away with something. Your job is, as much as possible, to help your teen experience the truth that relationships and life are better if she becomes more honest. Catch the deceptions that you can, but stay focused on the relationship.

You Can Do It!

Pray about your child's deception. God designed life to work better for us when we live in light. He wants your teen to reap the benefits of the life of love and truth that he offers: "Live as children of light."[27]

CHAPTER 30

Defiance

While defiance isn't pleasant, I will choose it over deception any day of the week. When a kid is in your face, at least you know where he is. You know exactly what he feels and where he stands.

Sometimes parents become intimidated by a defiant teen who yells or threatens. Before you give in to him, however, try this exercise: Imagine a three-year-old who is enraged because you won't let him have a cookie. See how his face swells up, and hear how he screams and stomps. Now paste your teen's face on that child. Now you have a picture of what you are dealing with. Does that help?

Defining the Problem

While they can appear similar, defiance and argumentativeness are not the same, and it's important for you to discern the difference. As we saw in chapter 23, an argumentative teen still accepts, at some level, your role as parent, while desperately attempting to make you change your mind. A defiant teen, however, questions or completely rejects your authority as a parent.

Sometimes argumentativeness escalates into defiance. This defiance, which flares up quickly and is emotional in nature, can lead a teen to impulsively say rash words. For example, "You are so unfair! I'm going to wear that dress whatever you say!"

While your teen sounds defiant, she may not be. The teen brain can't edit well yet, and your adolescent may not mean what she says. You probably remember saying similar things you didn't really mean and wished you could take back. So don't hold your teen to every word she says. Just say, "Well, I know you feel strongly about this, so let's wait till things are calmer and talk about it." This gives her some space and freedom, and it also keeps her from engaging in a power struggle with you. You want to prevent your teen from feeling the need to prove that she really meant what she said simply because she doesn't want to lose face with you. Saber rattling doesn't work well with adolescents.

True defiance, however, is not impulsive in nature. Defiant teens want to be their own boss, right here and right now, and prematurely fire their parents as their guardians and managers. Their battle cry is, "You can't tell me what to do!"

This thinking has some problems, of course. First, teenagers aren't yet ready to be their own boss. Without parents to guide and protect them, adolescents may be hurt or hurt themselves in some way because they lack maturity and do not have enough life experience to make good judgments. The second, and deeper, problem is this: *by design, we will never be totally and fully in charge of our own lives.* We were not created to be our own final authority. As adults, we all have to defer and submit, at some point, to other authorities in our lives. From God on down to bosses and supervisors and spouses, we need to respect someone.

So the adolescent's ultimate desire—to be in charge of her own life—needs to be shaped and matured into something more helpful so that one day she can become a functioning adult, with all the freedoms and all the restrictions of adulthood.

Handling the Problem

If you are like many parents, you'll find it difficult to deal with defiance. Defiance attacks your role as protector and can be emotionally draining. But if your teen is truly defiant, you must act, for the sake of your kid. Here are some guidelines for what to do.

Stand firm against defiance. Be reasonable and loving, but keep to your limit and be strong, as demonstrated in the following dialogue.

Defiant teen: "I'm going out the door and you can't stop me."

Parent: "You are right. I won't stop you. But please listen to me first. I want to work this out with you. Will you please reconsider?"

Defiant teen: "No. You are so unfair. I'm out of here."

Parent: "I have to let you know that this is your choice, and I'm not stopping you. But there will be a consequence, and it will be serious."

If your teen continues out the door, be sure you follow up. Don't let fear or fatigue or guilt stop you. Your teen needs to know that someone loves him enough to be stronger than he is, who can withstand his defiance, and who will give him external controls when he has insufficient internal controls.

When you stand firm against defiance, you are providing from the outside that which your adolescent does not possess on the inside: structure, self-control, respect for authority, delay of gratification, impulse control, and a host of other good skills. Your teen can then safely internalize these attributes from you so that they become hers.

Stay connected. Even though your teen's anger and rebellion against you can make connection challenging, as much as possible, stay in relationship with her. Take initiative to keep talking with your teen. Let her know that you are for her, even when she is defiant. Listen to her and validate her emotions. Keep in mind that in adolescence kids are trying to learn to integrate the darker and more aggressive parts of themselves. This is how they mature and become able to deal with failure, anger, and hurt in healthy and appropriate ways. If you can't be in relationship with your teen in her defiance, she won't learn to do this.

This doesn't mean you should subject yourself to abuse or injury. Always preserve yourself, but at the same time let your teen know that you want to connect.

Give as much freedom as your teen earns. If you have a defiant child, he will insist on total and complete freedom. Resist the temptation to remove all privileges and freedoms until he admits you are the boss. This plan often backfires, because the teen feels forced to take greater and greater power moves and to increase resistance. Instead, let your teen have whatever he earns. For example, ground him or take away his media. But don't do both if you don't have to.

Expect escalation. Expect your defiant teen to initially get worse rather than better after you set limits. This is the nature of defiance. Your teen is attempting to see how far she can go, and though she does not see it this way, she needs a parent who will stay firm and loving in the face of her increased defiance. Be stronger than your kid is. That is what a parent is and does.

Encourage adaptation and mourning. If this goes well, your teen will adapt to reality. He will give up the fight and accept that he cannot control everything and that he does have to answer to someone. However, he will feel some sadness that he can't have his way and that he must give up and surrender some fights and freedoms that he doesn't want to. Mad transforms into sad, which creates a functioning adult.

Seek professional help. If your kid's defiance gets out of control, get help. Sometimes a teen needs boundaries and structures that a parent can't provide. Counselors, youth pastors, school staff, residential treatment centers, and other intensive adolescent centers can support your values and the work you are doing. They can take your teen through the extreme times and help you become a better parent so that you can handle things when your teen returns.

You Can Do It!

Hold two pictures of your teen in your mind. One as a three-year-old without the cookie, and the other as an adult who can adapt to the authorities—from bosses and supervisors to God himself.

CHAPTER 31

Detaching from the Family in Unhealthy Ways

I was talking with Maria, a neighbor of mine. When I asked how her daughter Kate was, Maria told me, "Well, okay, I guess. Actually, I don't really know how she is. She comes home to sleep and eat. When you're a filling station, you lose touch."

Maria was trying to be funny, but I don't think she felt the situation was funny. She really wasn't sure anymore how her daughter was doing.

Like Maria, you may feel out of touch or disconnected from your teen, especially if your teen has begun driving. But is this a problem? After all, aren't adolescents supposed to begin separating and detaching in order to get ready to leave home? Isn't this to be expected? Maybe and maybe not.

Defining the Problem

If you feel disconnected from your teen, the problem may be yours rather than your teen's. You'll recall from chapter 12, "Separating from Parents," that adolescents are in the process of getting ready to leave home. This is normal, healthy, and according to their design. They are gradually shifting their interests, attachments, and allegiances to sources and relationships outside their family so that they can successfully leave home as adults. They can't be 100 percent connected both to their parents and to their friends, nor should they be.

So take an honest look at your feelings, and make sure you are not interpreting normal and healthy leaving as abandonment of or detachment from you. You love your teen and are attached to her, so it hurts when she begins moving away from you. You have spent many years of joy as well as craziness with her, and you are invested in what happens to her, so it's not easy to let go of the relationship you used to have with your teen, but you must.

Let it go. Take responsibility for your feelings of sadness. Look to others, not your adolescent, to help you grieve, feel sad, mourn, and let go. Don't make that your kid's issue, as she has enough on her plate already. And begin to let your teen go as well. She needs your blessing and your support, as the world is a scary place when you haven't been out in it.

However, even though separation itself is normal and healthy, not all adolescents leave home in healthy and normal ways. It could be that your teen does have a problem and isn't separating from you in a healthy way. If you see the following in your teen, she is detaching from you in an unhealthy way.

Emotional withdrawal. If your teen is withdrawn, distant, or cold, consider that a problem. A teen needs a warm emotional home base from which to launch so that he can be supported in his risks. Though he is not around as much, your teen should still be connected and present with you. Perhaps your teen is having a conflict in the family. He may be angry or depressed or even have a substance problem. Start digging.

Persistent anti-family attitude. Teens certainly have to challenge family values and relationships. But not all the time. Your teen shouldn't have a "friends are always okay, family is never okay" attitude. This generally signals unresolved issues at home.

If your teen is anti-family, confront her about it. Find out why she needs to keep you the bad guys. It may be that she feels it's the only way to get out of your control. Teens who feel enmeshed and smothered by their parents will often act this way. They need their parents to give them space, choices, and appropriate freedoms to help resolve their anti-family attitude.

Too much investment in the outside world. Sometimes teens are detached from home because they have become too busy with friends, school, and activities. This problem has more to do with an inability to structure their lives than with alienation. But too much investment can still be a real problem, as the teen becomes so busy that he can't get home for the support, connection, and stability he still needs. Such teens need help structuring their time better. They may not be mature enough to say "no" to attractive opportunities and need their parents' help to do that.

If your teen is detaching in any of these unhealthy ways, don't accept it as part of normal adolescence. It isn't, and your teen needs your help to change.

Handling the Problem

Here are some guidelines for what you can do.

Talk to your teen about your feelings. Let her know that although you support her activities and new life, you feel that you aren't connected anymore, and you want that to change. Let her know you miss her and want to be more caught up on her life, but this isn't about making her feel guilty. It's a heart-to-heart invitation that can help her move closer.

Ask about any negative feelings your teen may have toward you. Teens often shut down instead of saying they are angry at their parents, especially if the parents try to talk them out of their feelings. So go the second and third mile here. Ask your teen if he is upset, mad, or hurt about something you have done. Validate his feelings, and fix any problems you may have caused. This helps your teen deal with his negative emotions and feel safer about being closer to you.

Require respect. Teens sometimes emotionally dismiss their parents because the parents have not required the teen to respect them. When parents allow kids to become narcissistic and self-involved, the kids don't have empathy or interest in the lives of others, especially their family.

If your teen is self-involved, confront her about it, as it is damaging to her future. Let her know that you require her to listen to and care about the family, even though she's not around as much. If she does not make efforts, limit the time she spends with her friends until she gains respect for the family.

Schedule family time with your teen. In your kid's preteen years, family time didn't require a lot of planning. It just happened, as your child was more dependent on family. In contrast, parents of teens have to initiate some sort of structure just to stay connected with their kids.

For example, when I notice that I am not as in touch with my kids' lives as I want to be, I make them take walks with me. We walk around the block a couple of times, just the two of us. When they ask, "What do I have to do when I walk?" I answer, "Just talk about whatever is going on with you."

My kids sometimes resist at first, but after a few minutes, they will catch me up on their school activities, friends, and whatever they are doing. It works for us, for a couple of reasons. The activity, walking, doesn't distract from connection, unlike activities such as sports or movies. Walking also gives the boys space so they don't feel overwhelmed or smothered by me. They can be quiet, look around, and disengage a little until they feel ready to talk.

Schedule and hold on to family times. Keep them sacred.

You Can Do It!

Walk the tightrope between being emotionally available and yet letting your teen go. Your kid needs to know you are there.

CHAPTER 32

Disrespect

Not long ago a parent told me, "I cannot believe the words he used with me when I told him he couldn't go skateboarding! And that tone of voice, like he thinks I'm nothing!"

Another said, "There are times when my daughter and I are getting into it in the car, and she will be so mean and hurtful to me. Sometimes I will start crying. But I don't want her to feel guilty or like she has to take care of my feelings, so I hide it and continue the conversation."

I've often heard similar complaints from parents. Disrespect and teens seem to go together. If your teen has a problem with disrespect, it's important that you realize that disrespect often launches other behavior problems. For instance, teens who disrespect their parents' wishes that they not drink are only a step away from drinking. Teens who disrespect their parents' opinions about setting sexual limits for themselves are more likely to become sexually involved.

So as a parent, you need to understand disrespect and how to deal with it in ways that help your teen to mature and become a successful person.

Defining the Problem

Most people find it easier to recognize disrespect than to define it. Disrespect can be seen in a tone of voice, a body stance, or a rolling of the eyes, or it can be evidenced in choices teens make that indicate they aren't following their parents' values. Parents generally know when they are on the receiving end of a teen's disrespect, because it feels like an attack, and it is one. Disrespect is an assault on your place in the teen's life.

Rather than the presence of something, disrespect is actually an absence of something, *the absence of honor for someone,* for respect conveys honor. You show honor to people by giving weight to what is weighty about that person: their role in your life, their authority, their care for you. When teens disrespect, they dismiss that honor. Instead, they have contempt for or anger at a person, or they simply ignore the person. This lack of honor can be directed at someone as a person or at his or her feelings, opinions, needs, rules, or standards.

A teen's disrespect can be targeted at parents, teachers, relatives, neighbors, and even peers. When I am driving my kids and their friends around, I often have to say things to the latter, such as "You are being way too hard on Alex. It's not okay to talk that way to him. Back off."

Disrespect is rooted in several things that are going on simultaneously in your teen.

Self-focus. Teens tend to be narcissistic. They are less invested in getting along with the family unit and more aware of their emerging feelings and thoughts, which they view as theirs and no one else's. And those thoughts and feelings are strong and intense.

It's hard for teens to pay attention to what their inner world is saying as well as to what others are saying. So they listen more to themselves (and often those peers whom they admire) and less to others.

This self-focus contributes to disrespect. The more teens are invested in their own perceptions, the less honor they will give to others. Those around them feel negated and put down because the self-focus is so strong.

Power changes. Teens are coming into their own sense of power. They are smarter, more verbal, more mobile, and freer than they have ever been. Along with this increase in personal power can come a disrespect for others' feelings and thoughts. Because they are experimenting with being a stronger person, teens may not be as careful or kind about others, so people around them get annoyed or get their feelings hurt.

Authority shifts. Adolescents are also coming to terms with authority. They want to be their own boss and to be accountable to no one. Yet they are not ready for that sort of freedom, so they challenge, question, and argue with any and all adult authorities.

In itself this isn't bad; it is a helpful tension for the teen to resolve. However, it can lead to disrespecting a parent's feelings, wishes, rules, or values, which is defiance. (Defiance is directly related to the authority conflict, and because of its importance, it is addressed in chapter 30.)

Meanness. In addition, teens are experiencing their own dark side as part of the adolescent passage. They can simply be mean and cruel. It's a part of humanity that is certainly not good, but we all have the capacity for meanness. Meanness will often negate the respect and honor that a teen should give to other people. A teen may be sarcastic, attacking, or dismissive of others and not even feel bad about it.

Handling the Problem

You may be thinking, *This is a lot of stuff. Maybe I should just sit back and wait till he's out of the house.* Don't give in to that temptation. You can help your adolescent work through disrespectful attitudes and behaviors. Your teen needs for you to take part, and when you do, you can make a difference.

Here are five things you can do to raise the respect level of your teen.

Be a person who should be respected. Your kid should respect you, but you may be making it more difficult for your teen, particularly if you have unresolved character issues and problems, such as drinking, anger outbursts, self-centeredness, irresponsibility, people-pleasing, or a "do as I say, not as I do" stance, or if you depend on your teen to offer you comfort.

This bears repeating: Your teen doesn't need a perfect parent. But your teen needs to be able to look up to you and think, *That's what an adult is. That is a good thing to become.* In other words, become an honorable person with self-respect. This tells your teen that you should receive honor, and in turn, your teen will be more likely to become an honorable person as well.

Make room for differences and anger. Differences and anger are there, they are real, and they aren't all bad. Adolescents need to have their own feelings and experiences and to know what acceptable anger feels like.

Don't attempt to bring back the compliant nine-year-old you used to have, as you will be trying to force your adolescent to develop backward rather than forward, and he will (and should) resist it. Instead, make it all right for your teen to have his own mind and feelings. When your teen disagrees, say, "Interesting thought. Why do you think that?" This approach disarms much of the challenge and provocation.

I often cook breakfast to help my wife and give our boys a decent start on the day. To keep things from getting boring, I'm always figuring out new things to cook. One morning I made a special oatmeal with cinnamon and raisins. Halfway through, one of my sons said, "Dad, just to let you know, I don't like oatmeal."

"Okay, that's cool; thanks for telling me," I said. He wasn't being rebellious; he was stating a dislike. I don't want my teens to grow up saying they like things they don't and tolerating things they shouldn't.

Require respect. There is a difference, however, between differences and disrespect. Teens need room to differentiate themselves from their parents, but it can be done with honor.

Give specifics so your teen knows what is acceptable and what isn't. It may be that she honestly does not know the difference. Or if she does, your being specific will let her know where you are drawing the line. For example, say, "It's fine for you to disagree with me and even to get mad at me. That's how we know what we need to discuss and what problems we need to work out. But from now on, it's not okay to disrespect me. Here is what I mean by disrespect: rolling your eyes at me, being sarcastic with me, having a disrespectful tone of voice with me, raising your voice with me, swearing at me, or calling me names. There are probably more, but I'll let you know when you do them."

Tone of voice is always tricky because it's so subjective. But most teens understand what you mean by this. Their tone of voice gets them in trouble with their teacher at school and conveys contempt for the other person's viewpoint. But if your teen insists that she doesn't understand what you mean, then act out for her what she does. Make your meaning clear so that your child is responsible for the information.

Be an accurate feedback system. As the parent, you are your teen's primary teacher for learning how to disagree and have respect, so your feedback needs to be accurate and clear. If you are easily hurt when someone is direct with you, do some work on that. This is more your problem than your teen's, and you don't want him to be dishonest with the world because of what he learned from you.

But when your adolescent is being rude and disrespectful, confront him. He needs this information, so don't neglect giving it to him, even if it's inconvenient or difficult. Not long ago I was at dinner with some parents and kids, and one boy was in a foul mood, which he then directed at his mom, a friend of mine. He would say hurtful things, such as, "You're a crummy mom. You don't know anything," and she would divert him, saying, "How is your burger?" or "What movie do you want to see tonight?"

I didn't interfere, but later I told the mom, "Travis was all over you. Why didn't you say anything to him?"

She said, "Well, it wasn't that bad, and I was just tired of fighting anyway."

I understand being tired of fighting, I truly do. I could tell that she was exhausted by Travis. But no child should be allowed to talk to anyone like that. If your teen says similar kinds of things to you, something is wrong. Get help, support, and strengthening from other people, so that you can begin giving your teen feedback that a rude and disrespectful attitude is not okay.

Enforce consequences. If you have been clear about disrespect, but you haven't been imposing consequences up till now, expect your teen to test the limits. So have your consequences ready, and follow through with them.

Here is an example: "I talked to you about disrespect a few days ago, and I told you that you would lose a weekend night with your friends if you were disrespectful. Well, when you used that tone of voice with me at dinner and rolled your eyes, that was disrespect. You're grounded Friday night."

"But that's not fair!"

"I know you think that, but we've been over the rules, so they are clear. It's okay that you don't think I'm being fair, but I hope you don't make things worse by disagreeing right now in a disrespectful way, because I will ground you for a second night."

"But I didn't know!"

"Well, we've talked about it. And remember, I gave you a couple of warnings about it before I gave you a consequence, so that you would know. I think you knew. So if you don't want to be with me right now, you can leave the room. It's okay if you're mad, as long as you are not mad disrespectfully."

You Can Do It!

Freely and generously give your teen love and grace, and require that your child respect and honor you and others. In so doing, you will be helping your adolescent become an adult who treats others with respect.

CHAPTER 33

Driving and Cars

I wish I could say that every time I get in the passenger seat of the car to let my son practice driving, I experience nothing but pride in him and enjoying his development. But that's not all I feel. There is also some anxiety and even a little sadness. I think it probably symbolizes for me the growing lack of control I have over my son's life with each day that passes. This isn't a bad thing. It just is.

Defining the Problem

Here is the situation: someone whose brain has not yet finished developing, especially in judgment and impulse control, is operating a huge metal machine that can go really fast. Is this really a good idea?

Driving certainly puts your kid at risk of accident and injury, and she is automatically much more autonomous from you when she is driving. But at the same time, driving helps her continue developing her relationships with the outside world. Driving also gives her more choices and the opportunity to be responsible for those choices. If your teen is driving, you have to do less chauffeuring—and you have a very powerful privilege that she can lose at any time. So if your adolescent isn't driving responsibly, remove the privilege until she does.

For most parents, the driving problems they need help handling aren't about misbehaviors, such as speeding, accidents, and recklessness. Parents know how to address those concerns: take the keys, have the teen pay for her mistakes, and allow the police and courts to do what they do. More commonly, parents want an approach to the whole matter of driving. They want some guidelines answering three questions:

1. When should I let my teen get a driver's license?
2. How much should I let my teen drive?
3. Should I buy a car for my teen?

Handling the Problem

Here are some guidelines that can help you determine the best answers to these questions.

Require your teen to meet the basic requirements of life before getting a driver's license. Though most adolescents assume that they can get a license on their sixteenth birthday, you don't need to assume that. Licensure is a privilege, not a right. Just because a person has reached the legal age doesn't mean that she is mature enough to drive responsibly. You don't want a 140-pound four-year-old on the road.

So if your teen hasn't gotten her license yet, have the talk. Say, "I would like for you to take driver's education and get licensed at sixteen. But that depends on you. If you cannot choose to be responsible in other areas that we have discussed, I don't think you can be responsible in driving either. So I am requiring some things from you."

Then three months before your teen is eligible for driver's ed, establish a minimum time period of expected behavior. Set some reasonable expectations that have to be met. For example, require that your teen achieve a certain minimum grade point average and that she have no major behavioral violations, such as alcohol or lying, during the three-month period. If your teen blows it, the clock starts over, and she has to have a clean record for another period of time before being eligible again.

This is not about being punitive. This is the only time in your teen's life that you will have this particular leverage. She needs to know that it is a big deal and that your boundaries have meaning and substance.

Establish age-appropriate parameters. Don't allow your teen to drive anywhere at any time she feels like it. That will happen soon enough. It is a better idea to establish parameters that are age-appropriate and that you can gradually extend as your teen matures. For example:

Require your teen to meet certain reasonable requirements. Make sure she knows what your requirements are. For example, tell her she can drive as long as her attitude, conduct, and grades are acceptable. Also tell her she can lose the privilege anytime she crosses the line in these areas. But don't make perfection the requirement, or you risk discouraging and alienating her.

Require your teen not to have any driving problems, such as speeding, recklessness, or accidents. These are simply cause for losing the privilege of driving. If your teen loses her driving privileges, help her with whatever attitude is causing her to have driving problems. Inexperience? Poor judgment? Impatience? Does she feel omnipotent instead of careful? When she is upset, does she drive differently? Hold to the consequence and also help your teen resolve any attitude issues.

Require your teen to ask permission. Certainly in the early stages of driving, your teen needs to check with you before taking the car. This reminds her that the car is not an extension of herself, and it also allows you time to consider whether to grant permission. Take into account your teen's emotional state (she shouldn't drive if she's angry or upset, for instance); whether she's fulfilled her household responsibilities (are there tasks you want her to do?), and where she wants to go (a teen can go a lot farther away with a car than with a skateboard).

Require your teen to run errands. Your teen now has an extended capacity to do family chores. Use it! Send her to the store with a list of groceries to buy; have her pick up the clothes at the cleaners or get the takeout you ordered for dinner. She is learning to do things that she will have to do in a few short years on her own. In addition, she needs to understand that the family is a team and that greater privileges also mean greater responsibility.

Before you decide to buy another car, decide if it will meet a need. Are you considering purchasing another car to help out the family, or is it just to make your teen happy? The advantage of another car is that you don't have to share yours with your teen. But if your family doesn't do much driving, you may not need to buy another car.

Rather than buying your teen a car, consider getting another family car. If another car would meet a need, you might want to get another family car rather than buying your teen a car. There is a psychological difference between losing the family's car and losing "your" car. Should you need to take away your teen's driving privileges for a time, she will likely put up less resistance if the car she's been driving is yours and not hers.

Require your teen to pay some of the expense of the car. If you opt to buy your teen a car, then also have her pay for part of it with any money she has been earning. Give her a sense of the gravity of auto ownership.

And even if the car isn't the teen's, she is still the primary driver and can take some responsibility for the car itself. Require her to help pay a certain amount in order to help meet the expenses incurred for fuel, registration, insurance, and maintenance. Come up with a formula that is realistic for your teen, given his school responsibilities. If she has time to work, she probably should help pay for the car's expenses, as this will help her make the connection between a car and its expense.

You Can Do It!

Driving signifies that your teen is literally leaving you, for greater and greater distances and times, until the time comes when your teen will leave home for good. Help your teen prepare for that day by requiring her to be as responsible as she is free.

CHAPTER 34

God and Spirituality

I generally take a group of teens in my van to their youth service at church. I realized several years ago that my kids are less resistant to church if their friends go too. As they are getting out of the van, the last thing I say to them is, "Learn something about God."

After church I take them to a nearby hamburger place for lunch, but I don't allow anybody to get out of the van until everybody has answered one question: "What did you learn about God?" My standards are pretty low. I will accept anything that shows that a kid was listening. Why? Because spiritual growth comes from being interested in spiritual matters. If they show some interest, they have a burger. So far, no one has missed lunch yet.

Perhaps you are reading this chapter because your teen is resistant to, or disinterested in, spiritual matters. Maybe Sunday mornings are a battlefield because you have to fight your teen to get him to go to church. Or maybe your teen simply refuses to go to church with you.

If so, don't forget that God designed your teen to relate to him. Your teen has a vacuum inside that only God can fill. As Solomon says, "He has made everything beautiful in its time. He has also set eternity in the hearts of men; yet they cannot fathom what God has done from beginning to end."[28] God has set eternity in the heart of your adolescent. Whether or not he is aware of it, your teen needs God's love and truth.

But a relationship with God is something each one of us must choose for ourselves. Your teen will also have to choose, as a relationship with God can't be coerced. However, *even though you cannot make your teen choose God, you can expose him to God.* Teens who are exposed to God receive opportunities to experience, learn about, and be drawn to him and his ways.

Defining the Problem

As pointed out in the second section of this book, adolescence is the time when kids are trying to figure out what they do and do not believe. That means your teen is going to question you, your values, and reality itself. She is attempting to make her faith her own and not a clone of what you believe or have told her.

When your teen was very young, she likely had an identical view of you and of God. However, as she matured, she began to distinguish between the two. She has reached an age where she is more capable to see who God really is and to investigate for herself what spiritual issues are about.

This can be a disconcerting time for any parent. You pray for your teen, have spiritual discussions with her, and try to expose her to good spiritual activities. But in the end, she chooses God on her own, as we all must.

When it comes to spiritual matters, most teens have problems in three areas: faith struggles, lifestyle problems, and resistance to spiritual activities.

Handling the Problem

Let's look at each of these areas and at how you can intervene.

Be supportive and stay connected. When your teen says, "Why do I believe the Bible?" or even, "I don't know if I believe," you may feel anxious and concerned. However, statements like these indicate that your teen is invested and involved at some level in faith issues. He wouldn't say those things if he was dismissing faith altogether or was disinterested in spiritual things. Your teen needs to question his faith in order for it to become something substantial in his life. If he doesn't show some resistance to matters of faith, it's likely his heart is not truly involved.

Draw out questions. Find out why your kid is wondering what she is wondering. Listen. Don't make the mistake of giving quick-fix answers. Often they only serve to calm you down, and they don't help your teen. As the proverb teaches, "What a shame, what folly, to give advice before listening to the facts!"[29] Your teen needs a sounding board as much as she needs answers.

I often tell my kids, "You are having to figure out what you believe about God. I want to help you in any way I can. But I don't want you to worry that God is upset with you because you are questioning. He knows you are interested in him because you are questioning. And if our faith is true, it will stand up to your scrutiny. You are welcome to question anything."

It can be helpful to read books with your teen that are geared toward these matters. For example, Lee Strobel has written excellent materials for youth that answer questions about the Christian faith (*The Case for Faith*, Student Edition[30]) and the person of Christ (*The Case for Christ*, Youth Edition[31]). C. S. Lewis and Josh McDowell have also provided thought-provoking books that teens can grasp and benefit from.

Discuss how faith interacts with real life. Teens often struggle with integrating their beliefs with their practice. They are trying to work out their faith in the real world, and they will often stumble. Christian adolescents are wrestling with the same issues that all teens struggle with—for instance, coming to terms with their budding sexuality and fitting in with their peers. These issues provide opportunities for you to talk with your teen about what the Bible says about those things.

Let your teen know God cares more about relationship than about keeping score. Rather than pointing out those choices your teen may be making that are counter to our faith, show her a path that works for her. While you should always provide your teen with correction, confrontation, and consequences when needed, it's also critical that you help your teen see that God wants to support and help her with these concerns and that God does not want to condemn her.

Get your teen involved in a healthy youth group. The connections, identification, and peer support that teens get in good youth ministries are extremely valuable. I have known parents who have changed churches during their kids' teen years because the kids liked the youth group at a certain church. When your teen looks forward to church, you don't want to do something that might change that.

Insist that your teen join your family in going to church. It's common for teens to protest having to go to church or youth group meetings. Sometimes this is simply about authority conflicts with adults; other times the teen truly has little or no interest in spiritual matters.

I recommend this stance because when you take your teen to church, you are exposing him to information and opportunities to make spiritual choices. If your teen accuses you of forcing God down his throat, don't fall for it. Simply clarify that he can believe what he wants to believe but that he's going to church because that is what your family does.

In the later teen years, if your kid becomes adamant and a large power struggle ensues, you might agree that he doesn't have to go all the time. However, don't allow him to do something social or fun instead. Require him to be at home studying or doing something else that isn't entertainment.

You Can Do It!

A recent book, *Soul Searching: The Religious and Spiritual Lives of American Teenagers,*[32] concludes that parents are the greatest influence on the religious beliefs of teens. When you try to point your adolescent toward God, you are doing something significant and important.

Ultimately, however, issues of faith are between your teen and God. Your kid will decide what is true and whom to follow. As much as you can, support the search, give your teen as much exposure as you can, and get out of the way. God is doing his own work in wooing, connecting with, and drawing your teen to himself: "I love those who love me, and those who seek me find me."[33]

CHAPTER 35

Ignoring Parents

I used to think that if I wanted my kids to listen to something I said, I just needed to remove their headsets from their ears. That thinking didn't last long. I discovered that adolescents actually have the mental equivalent of an iPod deep inside their heads, and they can keep out anything you say for any length of time.

My kids seem to be able to hear words and sentences such as "Yes," "It's okay with me," "Allowance," and "You can go out tonight, " but they can't seem to hear "No," "Do your homework," and "Clean your room." It is a mystery.

Defining the Problem

All kidding aside, if you find that your teen doesn't listen to you, consider it a problem. She needs your input and guidance, and she needs to learn to listen to people even when she doesn't feel like it. After all, that is what grown-ups have to do in order to maintain their relationships and responsibilities. It can be helpful to remember this. Parents need to address this problem in teens, not because of their frustration with being ignored but for the sake of their kids' future success.

This problem is partly a developmental issue as your teen is gradually de-investing in you and instead investing in her outside world. You are becoming a little less central in her life every day. So don't expect your teen to relate to you as if you are the master, as a dog might. For example, when I get home, I am the center of my dogs' world, especially if I have food. My dogs will always have me as their Alpha, and they won't outgrow their dependence on me. That is the nature of the dog-owner relationship. But it's not the nature of the parent-child relationship. It's in your teen's nature to gradually make room for others besides you in her life.

Never lose sight of this reality. This is good for your teen. If she goes through this process successfully, when she moves out of your home, she will have a good support system and will be able to pick and maintain healthy friendships.

Also realize that most teens are so full of their own feelings, opinions, and experiences that they don't listen well to anyone—even each other. Sometimes the conversations teens have remind me of the parallel talks you hear in preschool:

"That teacher is so lame."

"Did you hear about Ann and Nick?"

"He gives too much homework on the weekends."

"They broke up. I can't believe it."

So you are probably not the only person your teen is ignoring. It just bothers you more.

Handling the Problem

Having said that, let's take a look at what you should expect from your teen when it comes to listening and what you can do to help your child to improve in this area.

Expect your teen to pay attention. Your teen may certainly be distracted by his inner and outer worlds, but he should attend to you when you talk to him. He doesn't have to agree or give you lots of feedback, but he needs to pay attention.

Talk to your teen about the problem. Sit down and be direct with him. Say, "Michael, it's hard to talk to you because it seems like you tune me out. That is not okay with me, because I need to connect with you. I don't want you to hang on to my every word, but I do insist that you pay attention to me when I want to talk to you, whether it be at the dinner table or in your room."

Also check to see if your kid has been alienated from you for some reason. Sometimes teens withdraw and shut down because they are hurt or feel misunderstood. This isn't so much a listening problem as a detachment issue. Find out if something between the two of you, or in his life, is causing this problem.

Expect your teen to acknowledge hearing you and ask for a response. Just because your kid is looking at you doesn't mean she gets it. Let her know exactly what she is to do so that you will know she is listening. For example:

"I want you to look at me when we talk, and I won't make it forever."

"I need you to say 'Okay' or 'All right' if you understand. It doesn't have to mean you agree. It just means you heard. It's not acceptable for you to sit there without responding. In fact, that's just plain rude."

"I need you to tell me what I just asked you to do, and by when, so I know you got it."

If you don't insist on a response, your teen can tell you, "I didn't hear you say that," when she doesn't do something you requested of her.

Hold your teen responsible for what was said. If you asked your teen to set the dinner table in five minutes and he doesn't do it, something didn't happen that should have happened. Say, "I asked you to set the dinner table, and you kept playing video games. This is not okay with me."

Give consequences if your teen continues to ignore you. You need to take the next step. Say, "I guess this is a bigger problem than I thought. I've asked you to pay attention to me when I tell you something and you must acknowledge that you heard me, and this isn't happening. So from now on, if you don't tell me, 'Okay,' and then follow through with what I've asked you to do, you will lose whatever is distracting you from paying attention, whether it's the television, computer, or music."

Don't expect your teen to be your confidant and listener. Sometimes parents want to tell their kid all about their life and struggles, as if the teen were a close friend. As you might recall from chapter 7, "For Single Parents," this is called *parentifying* the child, and isn't good for your teen. Kids who take on this role tend to have problems later in life, as they are unable to tell the difference between what they feel and what others feel.

While your teen does need to be able to interact mutually with you at some level, don't burden her with having to take care of your emotional needs. Use other grown-ups for that job. Your teen's life is so full and confusing that she can only take responsibility for herself. *Help your teen avoid having to avoid you because she feels smothered by your dependencies and needs.*

And don't feel hurt because you have to make your teen listen. It's not about you; it's where your teen is in life.

You Can Do It!

While it's okay for your teen to be more interested in his world than yours, it's not okay for him to ignore yours either. You are a part of his world and his responsibilities. Help him get outside himself and pay attention to you and others so that he can learn to how to relate to the real world.

CHAPTER 36

Impulsive Behaviors

Impulsive behaviors in teens can range from the goofy to the dangerous:

- going out tee-peeing after curfew
- hitting the guy who sits in front of him with a book
- burning hair off his arms
- getting in a car with a cute guy she don't know
- sticking her finger into an outlet
- riding a skateboard into a tree

If your teen does any of these impulsive behaviors, don't ask, "What were you thinking?" You already know the answer. If your teen had thought about it, he may or may not have done what he did.

Defining the Problem

You might recall from chapter 11, "Teens Think Differently," that the rational parts of the teen brain are less mature than the emotional and reactive parts, so teens have poorer judgment and impulse control. At the same time, their hormones are intense and strong, and they have feelings they have not had before. Adolescents are becoming more powerful, more curious, and more interested in trying out new things as they develop their own identity and place in the world. This is an unstable combination, at least for a time.

Impulsiveness is a sign of life. It signals that your adolescent has emotions and that she wants to experience life, take risks, and be present. In fact, a teen who doesn't have impulses may be struggling with detachment or depression. Adolescence is the time for impulses. So if your teen's impulsive behavior is sporadic and not serious, it's normal and nothing to worry about.

However, not all impulsivity is normal. When your teen's impulsive behavior interferes with relationships, family, tasks, school, or life, it is a problem. If it is getting in the way, or if it is harmful and not improving on its own, you need to help your teen.

Many of the problems we deal with in this book are impulsive in nature: aggressive behavior, violence, sexually acting out, drug use, and verbal outbursts. Don't assume your teen will grow out of these things. Many impulse-ridden adults are enslaved to their behaviors and have never grown out of them. Your teen needs your support and your structure to move her out of reacting and into using sound judgment.

Handling the Problem

Here are some ways you can help a teen whose impulsive behaviors need reining in.

Distinguish between impulsive behavior and character. First, realize that pure impulses are, by definition, thoughtless. They don't have a real and deliberate intention to them. They just are, like spontaneous combustion. But character issues are different. They do have thought and intention. A teen may be alienated, insecure, afraid, angry, or even cruel. He may not be able to express the words, but you can see them on his face and in his actions.

Some impulsive behaviors, such as the ones listed at the beginning of this chapter, can be silly or reckless, and others, such as violence, substance abuse, and sexual acting out, have more to do with character. As a parent, you need to pay attention to both types of impulsive behavior so that you can address any deeper issues along with the behaviors.

For example, suppose your kid is drinking. You have caught him several times, and you are now dealing with a big problem. Several things could be going on. He may be drinking because he craves the acceptance of his peers. Or he may be pushing against you and your rules. Or it could be that he feels entitled to do whatever he wants.

Combine any of these motivations with a vulnerability to impulses, and it is easy to understand the drinking. So don't just deal with the behavior. Make sure you are also helping your teen in his inner world.

Bring the problem into the relationship. As always, talk to your adolescent about her behavior. Let her know you are connected to her, even as erratic as she is being, and that you are not going anywhere. Make her aware of this problem, so that she has words and concepts to understand what she is doing. For example, you might say something like this: "I think you are pretty impulsive, and it is causing you some problems. I see it when you yell at me at home and when you get in trouble at school. When you act this way, it distances me and hurts my feelings. I am concerned that this behavior is going to affect you in even more negative ways, so we are going to deal with it and I am going to help you."

If your teen denies the problem or rejects your help, don't pay attention. Part of her is scared to death that she is out of control, and she needs someone to step in and help her get control.

Help your teen reflect on the behavior and its costs. Since impulses aren't connected to thought, bring thought into the scenario. Talk with your kid about what he does and what it costs him. Introduce him to the concept of reflection and judgment so that he sees what it looks like. Since your teen does not yet possess the ability to be reflective and to make sound decisions, he needs to see those things in you so that he can then internalize what he sees you do for him. This is how teens develop such capacities so that one day they can do it for themselves.

For example, you might say, "Remember this afternoon when you yelled at me for asking you to pick up your room? I am not angry about that, and I am not putting you down. But I want to give you a way to do this differently. When I ask you to clean up your room, I don't want you to say anything immediately. I want you to just listen and then think for a few seconds about what I said. If I'm asking you at a bad time, or if you have a bad feeling about this, then tell me, and we can talk about it. If you think you should clean up, that would be okay too. But I want you to start thinking about thinking, and I want you to *notice* what you are thinking and feeling."

If this sounds too abstract for your teen, simplify it. But the goal is to help him to begin taking ownership of his thoughts and feelings. This is the beginning of self-awareness.

Minimize external chaos. Kids who struggle with impulsiveness have a lot going on inside, and they can't make sense of it. They are internally chaotic. External chaos can exacerbate a kid's internal chaos. If, for example, your teen experiences you and your spouse having a lot of conflict, he has nowhere good to go with his own chaos. He needs to be living in an environment that is not chaotic. He needs love, support, structure, and order in his outside world.

So keep as much peace as you can around your teen. For instance, have regular mealtimes, keep the house in order, and put your teen on an appropriate sleeping schedule. These types of external structure and order will help him internalize the structure he doesn't have so that it becomes part of him.

Establish and keep the limits. Not only does your teen need your understanding and empathy regarding her impulsiveness; she needs for you to set boundaries for her. If your teen can't control her words or aggressive behaviors, don't ignore them. Such behaviors are not okay. Your teen needs to know that if she continues to do things without thinking, she is choosing to lose something that is important to her, whether it be freedom, social time, privileges, or some gadget. Be clear, and follow through with the consequence.

When kids with impulsivity problems experience appropriate and consistent consequences, they begin to develop the frustration, awareness, and self-control that will ultimately resolve the issue.

Sometimes a teen's impulses are so beyond him that he just can't stop his behavior. If you think this is true of your teen, keep in mind that the greater a kid's impulse problem, the more external care and structure that teen needs. So *increase support and structure to the extent of your teen's impulses.* This might mean anything from peer groups to counseling to another environment. (This last suggestion is for extreme situations.) Consult with someone experienced in these matters to help you determine the best course of action for your teen.

You Can Do It!

Self-control is not just a sign of spiritual growth.[34] It's also a sign of maturity. God designed teens to grow out of their enslavement to impulses into a life that he can be in charge of. Your job is to help your teen get on that path.

CHAPTER 37

Internet

Whatever you think about the Internet, as a parent you will need to deal with three realities:

1. It can be very useful to your teen.
2. It can be very harmful to your teen.
3. It is here to stay.

Some people estimate that there are now two billion Web pages, an incomprehensible number. The Internet provides your teen with access to tremendous amounts of research, news, and other helpful information. But information at that scale also brings with it problems that you will need to monitor and help your teen with.

Defining the Problem

When it comes to the Internet, you need to protect your teen from harmful content, harmful people, and harmful overinvolvement.

Offensive content. Pornography, extreme violence, and other anti-life information can be accessed on the Web. Sometimes teens will be exposed to images and text that are not good for anyone, especially a vulnerable teen.

Predatory or harmful people. Teens make online contact with lots of other people via instant messaging, email, chat rooms, blogs, and social networking systems. Sometimes they form unhealthy relationships with those they meet online. Teens can also be approached by those who prey on them or who will be a negative influence.

Disconnection from real life. Even when the information and connections are innocuous, teens can become overinvolved online. They can spend too much time on the computer and not attend to homework and other responsibilities. On a deeper level, they can also run the risk of living in the cyberworld and disconnecting from real-life relationships, activities, and experiences.

Handling the Problem

If the situation is serious, you may need to remove all online access from your teen. However, you can set some other parameters that can help you protect your teen while still allowing access to the Internet.

Know what makes your teen tick. Kids with Internet problems are vulnerable for different reasons. The more you understand your teen, the better you can help her with her own particular vulnerability. Some teens, for example, feel disengaged from relationships, and so fill up the void online. Others have little impulse control and are drawn to harmful material. Still others who are unhappy with their lives get on the Internet to escape.

So find out what draws your teen to the Internet, and help her with her weaknesses and vulnerabilities. While you can provide some protection for her on the outside, you will not be around forever. What your teen really needs is help for building up and strengthening what's inside her so that she is less vulnerable to unhealthy Web influences. After all, your teen will most likely be online when she leaves home. Help her grow and develop so that she is ready to use the Web responsibly when that time comes.

Talk to people with computer experience. Fortunately, a number of people and organizations provide information, answers, and software solutions to some of these problems. For example, there are ISPs and filters that can significantly reduce the amount of inappropriate content. There are also ways you can monitor your teen's talk time and connections with others on the computer.

Contact a professional computer service firm about these and other ways to lock out and discourage inappropriate Internet use and exposure. Even if your teen is more experienced in this world than you are, don't worry. Plenty of people know more than your kid. Talk to them!

Insist on safety over privacy. If your teen is using the Internet in unhealthy ways, his safety comes before his privacy and need for his own space and friendships. You may need to monitor what he does, either manually or electronically, with software that can do that. Once you see things getting better, as with anything else, you can gradually monitor your teen less and see how he handles the increased freedom.

Require life in the real world. The Web can draw you in for hours. I'm a grown-up, and I have lost track of many hours just browsing around. Teens are even more susceptible to getting caught up in the fascinating world of cyberspace.

Life and relationships were meant to be lived primarily person-to-person, face-to-face, and skin-to-skin. This is how we best operate and relate. So make sure your teen's life is centered on the real world. Insist your teen have "live" contact with family and friends, sports, arts, hobbies, musical activities, schoolwork, and church activities. When your teen is able to keep real life in the middle of her mind, she is better able to put her Web involvement in a subordinate position, where it can be the most helpful to her.

Set limits on when, and for how long, your teen can be online. It should not be during study time, as IM especially can be so distracting. Give her the time she needs to research what she needs to research, but don't allow her to do research as entertainment.

Establish the Internet as a privilege, not a need. Most of what your teen values about the Web isn't a necessity. It is more of a convenience. For instance, he can talk on the phone to his friends and listen to music on the radio, a stereo, or an iPod. He can even go to the library to use books instead of the computer to do research.

So don't be afraid to limit your teen's access to the Internet. You can remove or block applications such as IM and chat software if they become problems. (If you don't know how, ask an expert to tell you the steps.) If, however, you can't do that or don't want to, or if your teen reinstalls it, limit his computer access to times when you are in the room monitoring. You might even deny all access to the computer. If your teen reinstalls software you have removed, however, you also need to deal with the deception or defiance that is behind such a move.

You Can Do It!

If you have a teen and aren't computer-savvy, get some education in this area. The Internet is an important aspect of your adolescent's life, and the more you know, the more you can aid her in how to use it to her advantage rather than to her detriment.

CHAPTER 38

Money

When we were creating our allowance structure, Barbi and I told the boys, "You are now responsible for paying for your own social lives as long as we aren't present. If we go with you, we will pay." So now when they are broke, they sometimes invite us to go to the movies with them and their friends—as long as we sit in a separate section.

Defining the Problem

Money can talk to you about your teen. How your kid handles his finances can tell you a great deal not only about how he will handle them as an adult but also about how he will manage his life in general.

When you think about your teen and money, think of the word *future*. No other problem in this book is so clearly future related. Teens are generally oriented existentially; they live in the now. They think, *Tomorrow may never come, so live for today.* But if this attitude persists, your teen is headed for problems.

Credit card companies are lining up at colleges right now, waiting for your teen to arrive. They lure students to sign up for credit cards with the promise of instant gratification and "free money." Many college students don't understand the reality that they are incurring credit card debts that are beyond them. Will yours?

Most of the problems parents encounter with their teens are similar to the problems of many adults. They overspend. They buy things impulsively rather than deliberately. And they often borrow from friends and family and can never pay them back.

Many times these teens have an indulgent, conflict-avoidant, or maybe uninformed parent who is the true source of their problem. Parents are typically the source of their kids' money, and if the parents would stick to the limit, many of their teen's overspending problems would take care of themselves.

As a parent you have a lot of influence over your teen's attitude toward money. There are things you can do to educate your teen about money matters and to help him learn to save money and buy wisely.

Handling the Problem

Here are some thing you can do to help your teen become fiscally responsible.

Talk to your teen about money. Most teens don't have a good understanding of what things cost, or about saving, or about value. That's why the nation's advertisers target the teen market so heavily these days: so much discretionary income, so little judgment.

Until you tell her differently, your teen will likely be extremely unrealistic about money, particularly if she can get some from you anytime she wants it. She may even think that you get your money "for free" from the ATM.

So educate your teen about money matters. Give her some realities. Make sure she knows where your income comes from (no need to talk specific numbers), what you spend it on, and how you have to say "no" to yourself sometimes so that you can meet goals for the future, such as her college and your retirement. Help her understand how credit cards work, and teach her that there is no such thing as "free money."

Decide how the teen gets money. You want your adolescent to have an income so that you can help him become responsible for expenses. This may mean giving him an allowance, or having him find a job, or a combination of both. However you do this, have his income be more than fun money. It should be large enough, if possible, that he can pay for things that matter in real life, such as clothing, toiletries, social events and entertainment, just to name a few examples.

That said, establish a budget with him. Let him know that you will take on certain things for him and that he is responsible for certain things. If he blows the money on fun, he has less clothes or goes out less with his friends. Budgets are where your teen can truly experience the reality of fiscal responsibility, which can pay large dividends (literally) later in life.

Hold the line. Many parents don't require that their teens stick to the budget. The extra money has to come from somewhere, so many parents give in and make exceptions because they feel guilty or sorry for their teen, or they don't want to make their kid angry.

If this is you, I want you to think about the future you are helping create for your teen. Imagine her not being able to establish credit or get a home loan because of what she learned about money from you. Love is often saying "No" to "More, please."

Sometime parents loan money to their teens against the next allowance. They think, *Well, it's her money anyway, so what is the harm?* Plenty, I think. This sets up a dangerous credit mentality. So when your teen asks you for an advance, just say, "I gave you your allowance two weeks ago. You'll have to do what I do when I overspend, which is live on less for a couple more weeks. You'll make it, I'm sure." Give your teen the experience of learning that you spend what you *have*, not what you *will* have.

Set up a savings account for your teen. Not only do you want your teen to buy wisely, you also want him to develop a habit of saving money. Take him to the bank and help him set up a savings account.

Make sure the allowance includes some extra money—beyond your teen's expenses—that he can put into savings and then watch grow. You want him to develop the habit of putting a little away every time he gets some money, whether it's his allowance or a gift.

Set up a provision for giving. Also include some money for giving with the allowance. Make giving normal and expected so that generosity becomes part of your teen's life. When our kids were younger, Barbi and I deducted a certain percentage of their allowance for church and charities and just told them about it. When they became teens, we told them, "It's up to you now. You have to give something, but you decide how much." In a few short years they will be making those decisions for themselves, so we are giving them the freedom to decide part of this issue for themselves while they are still under our roof.

You Can Do It!

As a parent, you can use money to teach your teen how to take charge, be responsible, and have self-control. If your teen overspends, don't rush to the rescue. Allow your kid to experience the natural consequences of overspending. It will do wonders for your teen's attitude toward money.

CHAPTER 39

Moodiness

Jokes and giggling. Sudden wrestling matches in the living room. Affection and embraces out of the blue.

Doors slamming. Sullen silences. Negative comments and yelling about anything and everything.

These two opposite pictures can come from the same adolescent, often within minutes of each other.

Mood swings, which characterize the teen years, perplex many parents. Yet your adolescent goes through these moody patches for a reason.

Defining the Problem

A mood, which is basically a pervasive emotional state of mind, can be positive or negative, up or down. In most people, moods come and go, but they do not get in the way of love and life. They may wake up in a bad mood after a sleepless night or after an argument the evening before, but in time, the bad mood passes. Healthy adults have built-in stabilizers that sort things out—for example, the capacity to soothe oneself, the ability to have perspective, the knowledge that you can solve problems, and the ability to have hope.

But teens have not yet developed these abilities. Their insides aren't mature yet. Think of how a three-year-old views life. It's black and white, hell and heaven, agony and ecstasy. Adolescents tend to see their world in a similar way. While teens are more mature than children, of course, much more is being required of them. Teens have more complicated relationships. They desire freedom, yet they are still dependent. They feel confusion and instability, and so their ability to manage their moods breaks down.

Circumstances and environment do not control the moods of people who are mature. When mature people are under stress, they can eventually rally. When they achieve great success, they celebrate, but they take their success in stride. They are not what psychologists call "stimulus-bound." Their surroundings don't direct how they feel.

But for teens, surroundings mean everything. They live and breathe by what happens with their friends, in their home, and at school. Good events bring a euphoric mood, and bad events can bring a despairing mood. Sometimes a teen's increase in energy and activity comes from agitation rather than euphoria, and in time the energy and activity lessen.

But most parents aren't concerned about their teens' "up" moods. It's the sudden and abrupt shifts to the negative that concern them. During such periods, teens can't be talked out of their feelings. They may act out, and they may even blame their parents for their problems. The negative moods make life difficult for both the teen and those around them.

Often teens are much more moody at home than they are at school or with friends, particularly when it comes to their negative and down moods. This causes many parents to wonder if their adolescent is simply manipulating them. After all, their teen seems to pull life off pretty well in other environments.

If this is true of your teen, know this: your teen tends to be more down and negative at home because she feels safe with you. Home is where she feels she can be herself. Because of this, she allows herself to feel and express the more primitive and immature parts of herself when she's home. Yes, you are getting the worst of your teen. But your job is to help her mature and develop the abilities she needs to stabilize her moods by showing her acceptance and love—even while she is showing you the worst in her.

Handling the Problem

How can you help? You can do several things that can make a difference. Basically, do the same sorts of things you did when your teen was little. Here is what I mean.

Contain and empathize. In chapter 10, "A Period of Tremendous Change," we talked about the task of containing and empathizing with the strong emotions of a teen. You, the adult, listen, give compassion, and feed back the emotions so that your teen can then absorb them in a more meaningful and less extreme way.

You contain your teen's feelings rather than react to, invalidate, or try to change those feelings. You avoid saying things like, "Aren't you being dramatic here? It's really not that bad. Cheer up; it will get better." Your job is to be with your adolescent as he is.

This is how teens learn to regulate their moods. Remember, your teen's feelings seem larger than life to him and probably scare him. When you listen and put those intense feelings into perspective, you help your teen bear them.

Let me show you what this might look like. Let's say your fourteen-year-old daughter comes home from a party depressed and angry because of something that happened. To contain her feelings and empathize with them, you might say something like this: "Brooke, I know you're hurt by how Kelly treated you at the party. She got between you and your other friends, and it really embarrassed you. I can see why you'd feel sad and alone."

Your words have helped your daughter experience that someone else understands how she feels. But that's not all. They have also shown her a more mature perspective of what happened. If you had said, "Brooke, I would just want to die if Kelly had done that to me. I would feel like all my friends hate me and I can never return to school," you would have expressed emotions similar to what your daughter was feeling. But by not mirroring her anxiety, you are helping her internalize a more mature experience, and her negative mood should begin to get better. If it doesn't, you may need to offer some clarification.

Clarify. When you clarify, you give reality and perspective to your teen and her situation. You can counter her catastrophic thinking by giving your take on what happened. This can be very stabilizing for her. This takes some work, as you should not be patronizing or condescending. While you want to usher her into reality, your teen needs for you to respect what she is feeling.

For example, let's suppose that Brooke is still quite upset. You could clarify the situation for her by saying, "Brooke, you should be upset by what Kelly did. It was hurtful. At the same time, I want you to remember that the girls who are really on your side won't leave you, because you have some really solid and good friends. You are a good person, and good people like you, and will continue to like you."

Provide structure. Teens who are moody need an ordered, structured environment. Their internal world is unstructured, a little chaotic, and still forming. So they need their external world (you and their home) to be safe and stable. A good principle to keep in mind is this: *the more internally instable your teen, the more external stability you need to provide.*

So if your teen is having a lot of ups and downs, save your own ups and downs for other people. Make sure that you keep your promises and that you are consistent and dependable in time, scheduled activities, and meals. This, along with your warmth and support, can go a long way toward helping your adolescent begin to regulate his moods.

Keep the limits and consequences you would normally keep for your teen. Unless she has a clinical condition (which we will get to in a few paragraphs), don't allow disrespect, aggression, or acting out. Moody teens need a lot of love and comfort, but they don't have license to disrupt other people's lives.

Mention the mood only after containing, clarifying, and providing structure. Before you say, "I've noticed that your feelings are extreme, and I want to help you with them," try containing, clarifying, and providing structure first. This way you don't run the risk of causing your teen to feel invalidated and dismissed, so that she may not improve simply because she feels she has to prove you wrong. However, if your teen's moods don't improve over time, it might help to mention it so she can become more aware of what is going on.

Distinguish moodiness from bipolar disorder. Sometimes moodiness can be caused by a clinical problem. For instance, teens with a bipolar disorder experience extreme mood swings that disrupt normal functioning. They have a chemical imbalance contributing to the problem, and they need the help of a professional in order to improve. Good parenting alone won't be enough to help these teens improve. They need to be on medication to get stabilized.

If you have implemented the above suggestions, but your teen's moods are becoming more serious and she isn't responding, take her to an adolescent psychiatrist for an evaluation.

You Can Do It!

Don't be afraid of your teen's moods. Expect them, and deal with them. He needs a parent who will engage with him about them, talk to him, and help him. He needs a parent who knows what to do or else knows how to find someone who can help.

CHAPTER 40

Parties

Here is a transcript from a recent call I made to one of our kids while he was at a party:

"Hello?"

"Hi, it's Dad."

"Oh, hi. What's up?"

"I wanted to know if you need to come home early."

"Do I have to?"

"Yep."

"Aw, man ..."

"Pick you up in a few minutes."

"Come on, Dad ..."

"See you."

"Okay, bye."

This call was in code. "Do I have to?" meant, "Yes, I want to come home now." If my son had said, "Everything is fine," that would have meant, "I'm okay. I'll come home at the regular time."

From time to time, I will call and check in like this if I have questions about a party my kids are going to. I don't have enough questions to prohibit them from going, but I do have enough not to be totally relaxed either.

My phone call gives my kid an out if he needs it, but it still allows him to save face with his peers. In this particular instance, some kids had started drinking, and things were getting a little out of hand, and my son wanted to leave. And that is beginning to happen as they mature. That is the ultimate goal.

I don't want to give you the wrong impression. My kids and I have had many conversations in which they strongly wanted to stay, and I insisted they leave. Of course, I would prefer that they could directly tell their friends why they are leaving. But until that happens, I'll keep making the "mean parent phone call."

Defining the Problem

The teen party is quite a different entity from the primary school party. The latter is more about birthdays, the end of the school year, cake, and some planned activities. The teen party, however, more closely resembles a college party: it is about being together, music, and no planned activities, at least none that parents will be informed about.

If you have had problems with your adolescent at parties, it is likely that some of the following things have happened. Your teen

- drank or used drugs;
- got sexually involved;
- returned with a defiant attitude;
- left the party and got into trouble; or
- had contact with the wrong people.

These can be serious matters, and you will need to deal with them directly and seriously. Parties can cause an adolescent to regress. Peers, the fun atmosphere, and the lack of a strong adult presence can decrease a teen's judgment and impulse control.

Some parents don't allow their teens to go to parties in general because of the risk that their kids will be exposed to alcohol, drugs, and sex. If your teen has shown himself to be vulnerable in these areas, you may want to restrict him from attending parties until he demonstrates more self-control and responsibility.

Do teens need to go to parties in order to develop and mature? Of course not. Teens can become equipped for life without going to a party.

However, it's also true that safe parties can be meaningful and positive experiences for teens, full of good times, fun, connection, and celebration. Adolescents can learn about and experience helpful things about relationships when they attend good parties. And they will go to parties after they have left home, so it's much better for them to work out how to deal with them while still living with you.

If you are like most parents, you worry that you can't monitor events at the party. You know that bad things sometimes do happen at parties and that you will have no control over how your teen chooses to respond if the party becomes unsafe. Will your teen know how to get out if sex, alcohol, or drugs become part of the party? Will he know how to have fun and stay safe?

If you aren't sure, here are some things you can do to address your concern.

Handling the Problem

In order to maximize the odds that your teen will have safe and relatively sane party experiences, do the following.

Be clear about expectations and consequences. Tell your teen what behavior you require at parties. For example, you might say, "I want you to have fun with your friends. I know I won't be there to see you, but I still expect you to behave responsibly whether or not I am around."

Give your teen a few guidelines, some basic rules of conduct you expect your teen to follow, for example:

1. No alcohol or banned substances
2. No sexual involvement
3. No physical aggression
4. No leaving the site
5. Adult supervision required

Also, make sure that your teen knows that there will be consequences if she violates these basic rules. Make sure your teen knows that if she chooses not to live out these values, she will lose some privileges, such as phone use and computer time. She may even be banned from parties for a time.

Treat serious problems such as alcohol, drugs, and sexual acting out as issues in their own right. (See chapter 22, "Alcohol, Drugs, and Dependencies," and chapter 44, "Sexual Involvement.") You might need to consult a professional about helping your teen.

Talk to the host parents. I learned a long time ago not to buy the line, "Jamie's mom says it's okay." Sometimes such statements are lies; other times they are wishful thinking. Regardless, one of my basic rules of parenting is this: *Nothing happens until I talk to the parent.* That little rule has saved me many hours of grief. I have met some really nice parents by insisting on this rule, and these parents have always been appreciative of my call.

So call the host parents. Whether or not you know them, talking with them is a good thing. Ask them to tell you a little about the party, because you like for parents to be on the same page. Don't be weird, but at the same time, don't be afraid to ask them what is going on.

Here are some questions you might want to ask.

"Can I help?" Ask if you can help supervise or bring food. Your help is often welcome.

"Are you going to be there the whole time and be around the kids?" Sometimes host parents show up and then leave. Other times the parents stay in a different part of the house and never check in on the kids, so their so-called "presence" is useless.

"Are you going to allow drinking?" It's not a crazy question. Some parents have told me, "They're going to do it anyway, so it might as well be controlled and safe at my house." I think that makes as much sense as having condoms available at the party. Anyway, make sure you know the answer to this question.

"Is X or Y coming?" If you have some kids on your red-flag list whom you know are real trouble, find out if they will be there. It doesn't mean that your teen can't go, but you need to be informed.

Once you have this information, you may not want to let your teen attend, especially if the host parents won't be involved. If the answers reassured you, keep in mind that you now have some leverage with your teen. Tell her that a party is a privilege, not a right, and that her behavior in the days before the party will determine whether she attends.

Have a backup plan. Have some arrangement with your teen so that he has a way to back out if he needs to. You might tell your kid to call you if he needs to leave the party early. My wife and I have had to leave dinner early on date night in order to pick up our kids when they called, but it was worth it.

You Can Do It!

Don't be paranoid, but don't be in denial about parties either. Teens can have a lot of healthy fun at them. The more parents who require that teen parties be safe, the more safe parties there will be.

CHAPTER 41

Peers

The stoners.
The partiers.
The disrespectful.
The underachievers.
The aimless.
The rule breakers.

Your teen has some friends you aren't comfortable with. When you tell her your concerns, she defends them to you and claims you don't really understand them. What can you do?

Defining the Problem

Kids are highly vulnerable to their peers' attitudes and behaviors. Their peers can teach them about things you never wanted your kids to learn, and they can influence your teen to do things that are not only unwise but can be downright harmful to her.

Sometimes parents wonder if they should somehow find new friends for their teen and shut off access to old ones. While that might be necessary in extremely serious cases, in general this isn't the best course of action to take. If you resist the friends your teen chooses or block her efforts to make best friends outside her nuclear family, you are putting at risk your teen's ability to relate to a world that she will, sooner or later, enter.

Remember that God designed your teen to become more and more invested in relationships outside the family. His intent is for her to take the love, growth, and maturity you have helped her develop, and in turn give it to other people and in other contexts in the world. This is God's grand design, and it is a good thing.

But if you think peers may be negatively influencing your teen, there are some things you can do.

Handling the Problem

Here are some things to think about and take action on.

Determine if there is a problem. If your teen has a few questionable friends, don't take any action. Instead, look at the fruit of your kid's life. If he is loving and connected to you, if he is responsible and honest, and if his primary friendships are sound ones, it may be that he is being a positive influence on those questionable friends. Be aware of and pay attention to how your teen may be influenced by these friends, but that's it.

However, if you notice negative things happening from these friendships — your teen withdraws from you more, becomes more defiant, or starts having behavior, substance, or school problems — then you need to act.

Determine the attraction. Before you intervene, start figuring out what about the questionable friends attracts your teen to them. Let's say your teen has a group of good-hearted, responsible friends, but she also has some friends who have bad reputations. Why does she want to be with them? Here are some reasons to consider.

Your teen likes variety. Your adolescent may simply want different sorts of friends. He is figuring out his interests, preferences, and values, and so he is venturing out into other relationships. He wants friends who are studious, athletic, artistic, serious, funny, lazy, and rebellious. Your kid's friends can give you a visual of his insides. Monitor the way he is determining what kind of person he wants to be. (And remember the weird friends you had in your day!)

Your teen sees the good mixed in with the bad. Your teen may like the good aspects of weird kids. Adolescents aren't generally as afraid of the negative attributes in their friends as parents are. So your teen may like it that some troubled buddy is kind, easy to be with, accepting, or more honest than most. Your teen values the good she sees, while you worry about the effects of the bad.

Your teen is attracted to the opposite. Sometimes a friend represents a problem a teen is having. Who your teen is drawn to may tell you about some part of him that is struggling. For example, the compliant kid may gravitate toward the rebels, signifying that he wants more permission to disagree. The high achiever may hang with slacker friends as an indication that she is not doing well with the pressure she feels. The teen who doesn't feel approved will sometimes be with a dominant friend, who will approve of him if he does things the friend's way.

If you can identify the attraction, then you can help your teen work on his vulnerabilities so that he becomes less likely to be attracted to the wrong kids.

Talk to your teen about friends. If you see your teen's friendships dragging her down, talk to her about it. Tell her what you see and what you are concerned about. Let her know which kids you approve of, which you don't approve of, and why.

Should you tell your teen you want her to stop hanging around those kids? It depends. If possible, it is better to strengthen your teen from the inside while she is still in relationship with the problem kids. This enables her to do the internal work that will help her make good relational choices as an adult. Also, she is then less likely to feel forced to choose between you and her friends. Parents often lose on that decision, so it is best if you can be "both and" instead of "him or me."

Set limits on the amount and quality of time spent with troublesome kids. For example, you might say: "I know you like Josh, but I want you to know that I don't think he is good for you. I am not going to tell you that you can't be with him at all, because I don't think that is realistic. But it's not okay for you to be alone with him. In a group is fine; I don't expect you to walk away if he is with a group of you. But I don't want you driving somewhere with just him, for example. When you are with Josh, I want others with you."

If you are wondering how you could enforce such a boundary and whether it's a good idea to set a boundary you can't enforce, understand that having expectations about your teen's behavior is still a good thing. Besides, you're not telling your kid, "I will make you stop seeing Josh." You are saying, "I don't want you to be vulnerable to Josh, not because I want to control you, but because I care about you. Obviously, I can't know a lot about who you are with outside the home. But if I find out that you spent time alone with him, I will restrict your privileges. I want you to know that ahead of time." You are simply letting him know your expectations and the choices he has.

If, however, your teen is vulnerable and the friends he's hanging out with are toxic influences, you must rescue him from them. If you find that no matter what, your kid continues to struggle in major ways because of some friends, and your appeals and consequences aren't changing things, act decisively. You may even have to take him out of his environment and put him in a healthier one—for example, put him in a different school.

Ultimately, you want your teen to become mature enough to be around struggling kids and not succumb, because that is what adult life requires. So as soon your teen becomes stronger, give him a little more relational rope and see what he does with it.

Get involved. If your teen is deeply attached to kids you are worried about, meet those kids and talk to them. Get to know them so that you know who you are dealing with. You are letting them know that your teen has an involved parent. This can build some restraints into some kids.

And meet the parents. Call them and say, "Hi, I'm Taylor's dad. Taylor's a friend of your son, Danny. They've been talking about doing something this weekend, and I thought that since they're friends, maybe you and I could talk and get things on the same page." So many parents don't know the parents of their kids' friends. In my experience most parents genuinely appreciate the contact.

When my kids have gotten into trouble while around other kids, I have also called the parents to let them know what happened and to talk about how to respond. I have also talked to the teens themselves, so that they know that I like them but that I know the scoop and will be watching them for a while. My kids aren't crazy about this, but they put up with it. It's been interesting, because the kids I have talked to about troublesome behavior are also the kids I am closest to. They seem to appreciate and respond to me as an adult who doesn't judge them, who loves them, but who is also willing to confront them.

You Can Do It!

Remember not to make friends the core issue. Instead, focus on how your teen chooses and responds to friends. Don't force her to choose between her friend and you; simply help her feel supported and structured toward wise decisions.

CHAPTER 42

Phone

We signed up to try out an inexpensive family cell phone plan and have now become a wireless family. Everyone, including our teens, has a cell phone. My initial thought was, *Now we have another great consequence to leverage if we need to.*

This thinking had its flaws. We quickly found out that the cell phone greatly helps us keep track of the kids, wherever they are. And we became dependent on that assistance, to the point that the cell phone is not the first thing our kids lose if they disobey. And we are not alone.

One of my sons recently had his cell phone taken away because he was using it in class. The school requires that a parent pick up a confiscated cell phone, so my wife called to find out how and when to do that. When Barbi told the school secretary, "Next time he gets the phone taken away, we will suspend it for a long time," the secretary laughed and said, "Yeah, that's what all the parents say at first. But you need it more than the kid does."

Defining the Problem

When kids hit the teen years, they are inseparable from their phones. Preteens play together and do some talking. Teens talk, then talk about whom they talked with, and then they talk about when they will talk to someone else. Their internal push to connect with people outside the family, as well as their increasing conceptual and verbal abilities, finds expression in phone time. But phone usage can get out of control, so your job is to help your teen *learn how to master the phone, so that the phone doesn't master your teen.*

Phone problems revolve around excess. Teens tend to talk on the phone too much. If it's a cell phone, the time they talk means money. And no matter what kind of phone it is, if your teen is using it too much, she isn't attending to other things in life, such as homework, chores, and family relationships. Teens also tend to talk on the phone at the wrong times, such as during study time or when they should be sleeping.

Though it's easy to assume that phone excess is due to your teen's love affair with his social world, it may be due to other reasons. For instance, he may lack the ability to establish balance and self-control in how he spends his time. Or he may be avoiding some problem at home by connecting outside the home. Or it could be that he is simply self-absorbed; his world and experience may be the only ones that matter to him.

Whatever the reason your teen's phone usage is problematic, he needs your help to turn the situation around.

Handling the Problem

Here are some guidelines that can help.

Establish and enforce some ground rules. Talk with your teen and let her know what is appropriate and what is not. Your ground rules might include:

Life comes first. Teens by instinct want to answer the phone. When any of the phones rings in our house, the kids often feel compelled to answer. We have to remind them, "Use the phone as an answering machine. That's what voice mail is for." Teens need to get into the habit of not interrupting what they are doing simply because someone else wants to talk to them.

Some simple rules may be in order. For example:

1. Don't use the phone until homework and chores are done.

2. Don't pick up the phone if it is interrupting you while you are doing homework, doing chores, eating a meal, or doing something else with the family.

If your teen answers the phone every time it rings, she may have difficulty staying on task in work and in relationships. People get their feelings hurt when the person they are talking with abruptly answers the phone and gets into another conversation (this is a common adult problem).

The phone has a curfew too. Establish a time after which your teen can no longer make phone calls, especially during school nights. If he doesn't follow this, remove phone privileges as a consequence. It's a good idea to check in on your teen after lights-out, as it is easy for him to talk until very late. If necessary, take away your teen's phone at the cutoff time, and return it to him the next day.

When I call, I expect you to answer. When teens don't want their parent to know what they are doing, they sometimes don't answer the phone when the parent calls. Your teen needs to know that this is a form of deceit, and it's not okay with you. Let her know that if you find that she has been deceitful in this area, you will take it to mean she is not responsible enough to have a phone, and you will take away her phone privileges.

Limit the number of monthly cell phone minutes used. Many parents have become vigilant about monitoring their teen's cell phone minutes, and this is a good idea. Simply establish with your teen how many minutes a month he can have. Let him know that if he goes over those minutes, there will be a consequence, such as paying for the excess or being docked that many minutes in the next month. (If you depend on the phone to stay in touch with your teen, you may want to establish some consequences that aren't related to the phone.) In doing this, you are helping your teen see that there are built-in realities and limits to the phone and that they affect him.

I recently talked to one of my son's friends. He had just checked his minutes at the end of the monthly period and was elated that he had not gone over. But I don't think he would have cared about it if his mom hadn't cut off his phone after the months that he ran over.

His mom's consequence helped him create a sense of ownership and control over his phone usage. Now he cares, and the amount of time he spends on the phone matters to him.

Require phone etiquette. Your teen needs to know the basic rules of phone politeness, such as identifying yourself when you call someone. For example, she shouldn't call and simply say, "Is Pam there?" but rather, "Hi, this is Julie. Can I speak to Pam?" Nor should she say, "Bye," and then hang up abruptly without the other person being ready for the conversation to end.

Teens have different rules for each other, and that's fine. But make sure your teen knows phone etiquette, especially when she is talking on the phone to adults.

You Can Do It!

To a teen, the phone is a lifeline to his world. Hold your teen accountable for staying in touch with others in ways that demonstrate restraint and self-control. You may one day hear him say to a friend he's talking on the phone with, "I have to go study; see you later." That's the goal—internal control, rather than parental control.

CHAPTER 43

Runaways

When I was a houseparent at a kids' home in Texas, we had several teens slip out after lights-out and take off. Fortunately, the home was well organized and networked with the police and the community, and eventually almost all the kids were returned.

What amazed me, however, was how far the kids could get. Some would hitchhike many miles without being hurt. Although I was glad of that, they didn't learn from the experience in a "scared straight" kind of way, and several of them kept trying. The natural consequence didn't seem all that effective. Other things, which I'll cover in this chapter, provided much more help.

Having a runaway teen can be a frightening experience. Runaways are unprotected and vulnerable to possibly dangerous and life-threatening situations and people. While you shouldn't panic if your teen runs away, don't underreact either. Your teen needs the best you have so that you can help her.

Defining the Problem

Running away is *a premature attempt to leave home*. When teens leave home according to their design, they are moving toward something, and they have acquired the maturity, readiness, life skills, and support they need to meet life's demands. Not so with runaways. *They are more involved in going away from something than toward something.* These teens are running away in order to try and solve a problem that they can't resolve in any other way. On top of that, they don't have the necessary capabilities to face life on their own and can be in real trouble. Most have not thought out what they are going to do; they have only thought about what they do not want.

If you are dealing with a runaway, understand that the running away isn't the real problem; it's a symptom of another problem. Of course, you still need to keep your teen safe and protected. That is a given. However, the real problem is whatever is causing her to take this extreme step. What is influencing your teen to run away?

Most teens run away for one of the following reasons.

Home problems. If a teen lives with a raging parent, chaos, substance or sexual abuse, parents who are in major conflict, or similar kinds of issues, he may run away because he's overwhelmed and unable to deal with the problems. Home is supposed to be a place where a teen can sort out his feelings, changes, fears, and relationships in a supportive, accepting, and structured environment. But if a teen's outside world is as unstable as his inside world, he may feel that he has no choice but to get away, where he may find someone who can help him contain his feelings and thoughts and help him make sense of life.

Undeveloped coping skills. Some teens run because they don't have the ability to solve their own conflicts and problems. When this is the case, leaving is an impulsive solution to an unbearable situation. For instance, if a teen gets rejected and is treated cruelly by a group of people she likes, but does not have the social skills to restore these friendships or find new ones, she may run in order to escape the pain of feeling alone and disliked. Since the teen years are so intensely peer-driven, their rejection can feel like the world has fallen down around her.

Substance abuse. Teens with drug or alcohol problems sometimes run away in order to be able to continue their habit.

Sense of entitlement. Teens who feel that they should not be subject to rules and restrictions sometimes run away. They feel entitled to special treatment and demand that no one can tell them what to do.

This character issue comes out in small doses in adolescence and usually gets resolved over time.

However, if this sense of entitlement isn't addressed, a teen may leave home, which she perceives as controlling and unfair, in order to be as free as she would like to be. This classic adolescent fantasy never comes true, of course, because life doesn't offer absolute freedom to anyone.

Whatever the cause of your teen's running away, there are steps that you can and must take to help her turn around.

Handling the Problem

Here are some guidelines for what to do.

Get your teen back home. When you discover that your child is missing, immediately do everything you can to find him. Sometimes a chronic runaway has a few favorite friends he crashes with. Other times, he takes off with no place in mind except "away from home." If you can't find him quickly, call the police and report him missing. His safety is your first concern.

Get to your teen's heart. Your runaway is in pain. He may feel angry, misunderstood, overwhelmed, or afraid. But part of his heart has disengaged from you. Do your best to reconnect with that part and get it in relationship.

Don't begin by talking to your teen about how the running away affected you, as this can cause your teen to think you are blaming him for your feelings. Like many parents, Jesus' mother made this mistake after she accidentally left him on a trip. "His mother said to him, 'Son, why have you treated us like this? Your father and I have been anxiously searching for you.'"[35]

Instead, tell your teen, "I am concerned that you must be so unhappy that you want to leave. Whatever the problem is—*especially if it is something I am doing*—I want to know about it so things can be better for you. I won't get mad; I just want to listen to you. You must have a lot of bad stuff going on inside, and I would like you to tell me what it is."

Press on this. If your teen doesn't open up, tell him you'll have to take him to a counselor until he does open up. This has to happen.

Your teen lives in his heart; it is all he knows. Do all you can to get to that place deep inside him.

Change whatever you need to change. If your teen ran away because of problems in your home, take an aggressive stance to make it more tolerable to her. Every home has some problems, but do all you can so that your teen doesn't have to experience the brunt of them. If you and your spouse are having conflicts, make sure your teen doesn't observe them.

Remember, adolescents by nature have plenty of their own internal chaos, and they need home to be a place where they feel safe, loved, and listened to. Your teen has many feelings and experiences that she needs your help containing. Depend on friends and support outside the home to help you deal with your own struggles so that you can make peace and space for your teen. As an adult, you have some options to deal with your issues, but *you* are your kid's primary source of help.

Have requirements. Tell your teen, "I am working on listening to you so that I understand why you ran away, and so I can help solve the problems. But at the same time, running away isn't okay. It's dangerous, and you could get really hurt, so I can't allow it. I want you to be patient and stick with me while we deal with your unhappiness and whatever I am doing to cause it. If you feel like running, let me know and we can talk about it. But if you leave again, I will have to set consequences with you to keep you safe. I don't want to do that, but I will. So please keep the lines open as much as you can."

Give as much additional structure as needed. If your teen still appears to be a runaway risk, despite your best efforts to listen and address the causes of his running way, bring in additional resources. Adolescent counselors are trained to help, and out-of-home living environments can also make a difference.

The purpose of this additional structure is to protect your teen while working with him on the underlying causes of his running, so that ultimately, he can come home, then leave home at the right and appropriate time: ready and equipped for life as an adult.

You Can Do It!

When dealing with a runaway teen, you can feel unappreciated, but you aren't. You are trying hard to love your teen, who, for some reason, doesn't want to be around you. This reality calls on you to be the best parent you can be. Your highest calling as a parent is to do the right thing by a kid who is hating you the entire time. God does this every day for us: "He is patient with you, not wanting anyone to perish, but everyone to come to repentance."[36] Stay the course, and connect with the unhappiness. Your teen needs you.

CHAPTER 44

Sexual Involvement

The phrase "rainbow party" recently made the rounds in high school circles. It refers to parties where each girl in attendance applies a different shade of lipstick and then performs oral sex on each boy. While the prevalence of these parties may be debated, their existence is one of many examples of the increase in sexual involvement among adolescents. Sexual behavior that used to be considered unacceptable is now acceptable.

Defining the Problem

As the parent of a teen, you must accept the reality that this kid, whom you raised from a baby, is now a very sexual being. His body is ready for sex. He thinks about sex and talks about sex—and a large part of him wants to be having sex. Some parents find this reality easier to accept than others, but you must make this mental shift so that you can best help your teen navigate through the waters of adolescent sexuality.

Everyone knows that a lot of teens are having sex and are experiencing the consequences: emotional hurts, pregnancies, and diseases. But because teens tend to hide their sexual activity from their parents, parents often find out about it only after the problems have already arisen.

There are several reasons why adolescents engage in sexual activity:

1. Biologically they are ready for sex, and their hormones are raging.
2. Many of their peers are sexually active, and the culture supports sex as being okay for teens.
3. They don't value abstinence or virginity.
4. They have weaknesses and vulnerabilities that make them susceptible in this area. (See chapter 22, "Alcohol, Drugs, and Dependencies," for more information about this.)

If this feels overwhelming to you, imagine how it feels to your teen. He has to deal with his sexuality himself. So if you find out that your teen has engaged in sexual activity of some sort, don't overreact or try to control your teen. Instead, follow these guidelines.

Handling the Problem

Here are some things you can do to make a positive difference in your teen's sexual choices, whether or not your teen has already acted out sexually.

Have "The Talk" and keep on talking. Talk about sex with your teen, and more than the required one about the birds and the bees. Bring it up often so that it becomes a comfortable topic of conversation between the two of you.

Your teen may not act like she wants to have these conversations with you, but never mind that. Even if she thinks she knows all that she needs to know (from friends, the Internet, or other not-so-healthy sources), your teen needs to hear from you on this subject.

Make sure your teen understands the following:

1. God made us sexual beings, and anything God created is good.
2. Sexuality is more than sexual behavior. We relate to the world and others as a sexual being, in sexual ways. Our sexuality is part of who we are.
3. Boys relate sexually in different ways than girls do. This is all part of God's grand design.

4. Sexual fulfillment is meant to be experienced in marriage, and when it is experienced in that relationship, it can deepen intimacy and love.

In addition, help your teen understand that virginity is a gift to one's future spouse, and so she needs to set appropriate physical limits to protect her virginity. Talk with her about what those limits might be, and give her the reasons for those limits. It is just not enough to tell teens, "Don't do it." They need meaningful reasons to abstain, especially in today's culture. Discuss the personal and spiritual reasons for abstaining, as well as the natural consequences of sexual activity, such as diseases and unwanted pregnancies.

Most of all, touch your teen's heart in the area of sexuality. As much as you can, connect with her feelings and fears so that she knows you are on her side. Sex is a very private and personal matter, and your teen is likely to hide her sexual life from you. There is a lot you may never know about this part of your child's life, so your goal needs to be that your teen internalize healthy values and standards when it comes to sex. If your goal is to prevent your kids from having sex, you have lost the big picture of parenting. Far better for your teen to value sexual abstinence, respect, and self-control because she thinks they are important and the best way for her.

If you aren't used to talking about this subject with your teen, it can be awkward for both of you. But you need to do it. This topic is too important to hand off to someone else. Get in touch with other healthy parents, youth ministries, and teen experts to help you find ways to talk in the most natural ways possible. (See the sidebar for a list of books that can help you talk with your teen about sexual matters.)

Listen and find out what is really going on. Your teen needs you to teach him about sex and about your values. Equally important is that you help your teen grow and mature in his character.

Your teen has feelings, experiences, and fears about sexuality. Draw out what he is dealing with when it comes to sex. Ask about what's going on with him, with his friends, and with other kids at school. He may be waiting for you to take the initiative.

Like adults, teens use sexuality as a way of dealing with their emotions and problems. Determine what your teen might be struggling with. Sometimes sexual acting out is a symptom of impulsivity and a general lack of self-control. If this is the case, talk to your teen about learning patience, diligence, and delay of gratification in all walks of life.

If your teen has problems being close and vulnerable with others, he may use sexual activity as a way to experience closeness without the risk of emotional intimacy. If so, your teen needs help in learning to open up emotionally. Offer him support, and guide him into the world of intimacy and relationships so that he doesn't need the shortcut.

If your teen is using sex to medicate hurt, rejection, or self-image problems, dig underneath his life to where he really lives, and help him solve these underlying issues that are causing him to act out so that he can heal and become stronger inside. (A great reference for what makes kids tick is Dr. Cloud's and my book *Raising Great Kids.*[37])

Confront any sexual activity you know about. If you learn that your teen is acting out sexually, confront it. She is probably in way over her head and needs your help to get out. Let your teen know that you know and that you are concerned for her.

Most teens will listen to their parents if the parents don't overreact or condemn them. It's likely that part of your teen knows she is hurting herself, and she just needs someone to support her own boundaries. If this is the case, keep an open line with her and help her. Offer practical suggestions, such as finding a healthy peer or youth leader to support her and hold her accountable in this. Help her establish a boundary, such as not spending time alone with a date, and give her wholesome social activities to fill the void.

Friends, music, magazines, television, and movies can all pressure your teen to have sex. Let her know that you will help her stand against those pressures, so she can maintain her sexual purity and her physical, emotional, and spiritual health.

If you encounter defiance and resistance, establish consequences, such as loss of your teen's social freedoms, which are being misused. Don't focus on the girlfriend or boyfriend, as the other person is not the issue. Your teen's values about sexuality are the issue. If you make it about the other person, both teens may feel persecuted by you, and this may bind them closer together.

What about masturbation? It may be awkward for you to think about as the parent, but remember your own adolescence again. It's part of life. The great majority of teens (virtually all boys and many girls) will masturbate. There is no negative medical or health issue related to this. However, it is something that your teen may feel guilt or shame about. Talk to him and let him know that there is no condemnation from you or God about this. At the same time, if you suspect that the masturbation is serving as a way to handle stress, problems, and loneliness, or if he is in danger of a pornography dependence, he needs your help. Tell him your concern and help him find ways to open up and deal with his problems, fears, and issues in more productive ways.

Finally, if your teen has had sex and struggles with guilt or the feeling of being damaged goods, help her know about God's grace and forgiveness. He is truly the God of second chances. Your adolescent needs to know that God and you love and accept her and want to help her find help, hope, and a new start: "In him we have redemption through his blood, the forgiveness of sins, in accordance with the riches of God's grace."[38]

You Can Do It!

When you walk alongside your teen into the uncomfortable world of sexuality, you are being the courageous shepherd and guardian of your child that God intended. Guide your child into understanding and experiencing sexuality as God designed it: healthy, loving, and self-controlled.

BOOKS FOR TEENS

Stephen Arterburn and Fred Stoeker, with Mike Yorkey, *Every Young Man's Battle* (Colorado Springs: WaterBrook Press, 2003). Shows young men how to train their eyes and mind, how to clean

---

up their thought life, and how to develop a realistic battle plan for remaining pure in today's sexually soaked culture.

Dr. Henry Cloud and Dr. John Townsend, *Boundaries in Dating* (Grand Rapids: Zondervan, 2000). The chapter called "Set Appropriate Physical Limits" provides the spiritual and relational background for establishing good sexual boundaries, such as becoming holy, having self-control, not being enslaved to lust, and having healthy relationships with others and with God.

Shannon Ethridge and Steve Arterburn, *Every Young Woman's Battle* (Colorado Springs: WaterBrook Press, 2004). Offers guidance for how to experience frank, thorough, and natural conversations with your daughter about sexuality and sexual integrity.

BOOKS FOR PARENTS

Stephen Arterburn, Mike Yorkey, and Fred Stoeker, *Preparing Your Son for Every Man's Battle* (Colorado Springs: Water-Brook Press, 2003). Offers guidance for how to experience frank, thorough, and natural conversations with your son about sexual integrity.

Shannon Ethridge, *Preparing Your Daughter for Every Woman's Battle* (Colorado Springs: WaterBrook Press, 2005). Offers guidance for how to experience frank, thorough, and natural conversations with your daughter about sexuality and sexual integrity.

CHAPTER 45

Silence

Parker is so quiet. It really bothers me. I feel like I'm losing touch with him."

I was talking with Renee, Parker's mom, at the grocery store. Her son had always been quiet, but now that he was a teenager, he hardly talked at all.

"Is he mad at you?" I asked.

"I don't know. He doesn't seem mad. He just doesn't say anything."

I didn't think about the conversation again until our families got together a few weeks later. Then my eyes were opened as to the reason for Parker's withdrawal.

Walking over to him, I asked, "So, how is baseball going?"

"Pretty good; my swing is ..."

"His swing is better than it was last year, now that he's getting lessons," Renee interrupted.

As his mom was speaking, I watched Parker withdraw.

I began again: "So, how are the lessons going?"

"Well, he's working with me on my stance because ..."

"Because he stands away from the plate and loses power."

Again, I saw Parker pull away inwardly.

As I watched Renee interrupt her son and speak for him repeatedly over the course of the evening, I felt I had to do something. The next time she interrupted Parker, I looked directly at him and said, "Parker, I want to hear this from you."

I talked with Renee later about what I'd observed. She hadn't realized how much she ran over Parker, and she didn't like what she was doing. She realized that in constantly speaking for her son, she was discounting and devaluing him as an individual who had his own opinions and feelings.

Defining the Problem

Parents are sometimes dismayed and worried that their chatty ten-year-old has become a withdrawn fourteen-year-old. However, many times a teen's silence is due to adolescence rather than a problem with him or with the parent.

Silence is a necessary and healthy part of the transition into adulthood. Teens need to create a place in their mind that their parents do not occupy. They have to clear room so they can separate others' emotions and thoughts from their own. Silence is like random access memory (RAM), the part of the computer used by programs to perform tasks. Silence provides the thinking space teens need in order to sort out what and who they are.

Remember, too, that adolescents prepare for adulthood by withdrawing from their families and engaging more with the outside world. If parents can give teens freedom, love, and acceptance, they will come up for air and relate again to the family. However, their views will be their own and they probably will not share every thought and feeling as they often did when they were young.

But as Parker's mom discovered, sometimes a teen's silence does indicate a problem. If your teen's silence is caused by any of the following reasons, it isn't normal or healthy and is cause for concern.

Withdrawal from an intrusive parent. When parents interpret their teen's silence as either a withdrawal of love or a serious problem, they sometimes overwhelm the teen with words. This can hinder a teen's ability to have her own experiences. By being overly intrusive, the parent creates an actual problem and perpetuates a cycle of interrogation and withdrawal.

Limited ability to describe experiences and emotions. Teens sometimes don't have a vocabulary adequate to describe their experiences, feelings, and reactions. They are much more comfortable simply commenting briefly on their activities. Emotion-laden words, such as *sad*, *angry*, *confused*, *hurt*, and *scared*, aren't as comfortable for them, and so teens often avoid using them. They experience these emotions, but they don't find them easy to articulate and express.

Fear of emotion. Even when they have the emotional vocabulary, teens often prefer to avoid dealing with strong negative feelings. They are still working on experiencing emotions without being afraid the emotions might get out of control or become too painful to bear. In response, the teen shuts down. The emotions don't go away, but the teen is, temporarily, spared his fear and anxiety about what might happen inside himself.

Depression. Teens who are depressed are often silent. Depression is painful; often a depressed teen feels as if everything is wrong with her and her life; she has lost hope for anything good. Often she will withdraw from her parents, and sometimes the world, as a way to manage very strong emotions with which she is unable to deal.

Passive punishment. At times teens withdraw into silence because they feel angry or hostile toward their parents and don't want to risk incurring their parents' anger with angry words or actions. Instead, they withdraw in passive retaliation toward real or perceived mistreatment. Their silence conveys anger, dismissal, or contempt.

Handling the Problem

Fortunately, with the right understanding and patience, parents can make significant inroads with a silent adolescent. Here are some suggestions.

Talk about the root of the silence. You might be tempted to talk first about the silence itself; however, your teen lives and focuses more on the problems that shut him down. So first address the reason behind the silence, whether it be punishment, depression, fear, or withdrawal from intrusiveness.

Discuss the silence. Once you've discussed the reason for the silence, bring up the silence itself. You might say, "I'm glad we talked about how mad you are with me for grounding you. It's really hard for me when you shut down. I can't tell where you are, and I don't know what to say or what will help. I need you to let me know when you are upset and not just remain quiet. You may not even know when you are doing this, but it happens pretty frequently. If you aren't aware of when I need to hear from you, I'll let you know so we can talk about it. Okay?"

Give space and time. Remember that even when life is going well, your teen may be reserved. Don't force chatty connectedness and press her inside herself again. Instead, allow enough space and time for her to assimilate what has been said and done so far. You want your teen to come out of her silence because she wants to, not because she feels coerced.

Require dialogue. You may need to go beyond invitation to expectation. This is truer with teens who are angry and punishing than with those who are hurt or running. The latter tend to need more problem solving and connecting. For example, you might tell your teen, "I'll do everything I can to change the things I do that make it hard for you to talk to me. I don't need you to talk all the time about everything, but I do need you to talk to me—if not on your own, at least when I want to know how you are doing. I need you to have real conversations with me because I love you and care about you. If you refuse to talk, you are telling me you don't take your responsibilities for being in our relationship seriously, and there will be consequences."

Whatever consequences you establish, remember they are for the purpose of helping your teen open up. When he makes the effort to dialogue, drop the consequence and connect.

You Can Do It!

Dealing positively with silence takes work. At the same time, the lessons you teach your teen about handling difficult situations through alternatives to silence will help guide her through future relationships.

EPILOGUE

Whenever I hear that some young adult whom I knew as a teen is doing well, I always get this sense of celebration. *Attaboy!* I also have a sense of relief. *Well, I guess there's hope for the world after all.* Just recently I heard that two are getting married, another has been promoted in his organization, and still another is finishing a grad degree. How did they go from where they were to where they are now? It's proof God exists.

Every successful person in the world, young or old, was once a teen. They all went through the fire. Probably drove their parents to distraction. Made horrible mistakes. Showed little indication that they would ever amount to anything. And yet, they came out on the other end of the adolescent passage and have taken their seats in their proper places in the world, including dating, marriage, career, and even their own ventures into parenting.

Remember this reality during these crazy years. It is so easy to live in the crisis of the day. While crises must certainly be dealt with, don't remain stuck in today's problem. That is where your teen lives, and you need to be the one who pulls her out of the crisis by your love and greater sense of perspective.

Your teen needs you. Period.

She may not show it, but she is jumbled up inside and unable to function as she should on the outside. She needs a loving, accepting, and validating parent to center her mind and heart and help usher her into the adult world. Do the work of drawing out your kid's feelings and thoughts, especially the troubling ones, and help her bring her fears, failures, and frustrations to the light of relationship, where they belong and can be matured.

So where do you go from here?

Live a life of love and structure. Time alone never healed anything, regardless of the old saying. Time plus grace plus truth can heal just about everything. So don't wait, but take the reins of parenthood and start riding.

The more you integrate boundaries as part of your everyday life and relationships, the more normal these structures will become for your teen. It may be an adjustment at first, moving from rescuing or ignoring to confronting and following through with consequences. But the more you keep at it, the more likely it is that your kid will adapt, become more responsible, consider the feelings of others, and develop awareness and self-control.

Work on your own growth. Being responsible for adolescents tends to expose our weaknesses in a way that few experiences do. I never knew I had a temper until my teens showed it to me. Now they remind me of it often.

Find a way to grow and work on those weaknesses and areas of yourself that need to mature or heal. Get involved in a healthy church, a small group, or a parents of teens support group, or find a spiritual director or a good therapist. When you work on character issues, you are also working on parenting issues, because parenting is all about your own character. As you get healthy, so does your parenting. So get in touch with people who are mature, loving, and truthful—and make use of what you learn.

Seek God. God is personal, emotional, and present with you and your teen. Teen angst doesn't confuse or frustrate him at all. In fact, as the Designer of the adolescent passage, he has wisdom, guidance, grace, and encouragement for you. Follow him, seek him, and ask for his life within you. God is in the business of redeeming a world that needs him, and all the parts of your teen's life need that redemption, for we are only totally complete when we connect with him. Ask him for life and light for the both of you. As the Bible says, "For with you is the fountain of life; in your light we see light."[39]

Keep your teen's future in sight. *You are your kid's best hope for becoming a loving, functioning, and successful adult. You,* the loving and strict parent whom he loves and hates, but ultimately needs, at a very deep level.

Your teen is moving quickly toward his future. In just a few short years he will be leaving you to take his place in the world. What can you do, even today, to help your teen become a grown-up who will prosper and give good things to others?

As a parent, you have no greater task, and no higher good.

God bless you and your teen.

Dr. John Townsend
Newport Beach, California

APPENDIX A

Seeking the Help of a Professional

Parents of teens often feel confused about knowing how and when to look for professional help. Are we overreacting? What if it will all go away? Fortunately, adolescent therapy can be very helpful and successful these days, and there are some good guidelines for knowing what to do.

When Should I Seek a Therapist's Help?

You should seek professional help when:

Your teen is in crisis. Problems such as drug use, serious violence, cutting or burning, and thoughts of hurting oneself require someone with experience who can keep your teen out of danger.

All other attempts haven't worked. These include your own interventions, support, guidance, encouragement, rules, and consequences. They may also include the school system and your church's youth leaders. If you have tried various avenues and given your teen a reasonable amount of time to change, but change hasn't occurred, it's likely time to bring in a professional.

How Can I Find a Good Therapist?

The best way to find a good therapist is to ask the people who frequently refer adolescents to see therapists. For example, school counselors and youth pastors likely know of good adolescent specialists in your area. Because of their work with teens and families, they get feedback about which counselors can effectively work with teens struggling with specific issues. Find the gatekeepers and get their advice.

I also recommend that your teen undergo a complete medical exam. Some behavioral problems can be influenced or worsened by underlying medical or biological issues, and your teen may need to be treated by an adolescent psychiatrist or a physician who is experienced in adolescent problems. Issues such as attention deficit disorder (ADD), attention deficit hyperactivity disorder (ADHD), and bipolar disorder may improve significantly with the correct medications, and these improvements can translate to improvements in behavior and attitudes.

Tips for When You Don't Know What to Do

You can't plan for every situation. Things will come up that you are not ready for, yet you must do something to help your teen. Here is a list of tips to assist you in those moments when you have no idea what to do.

When in doubt, try to connect with your teen. Don't argue, keep reasoning, or start threatening when it's clear that you aren't getting anywhere. Just stop and try to make a connection. This can solve a multitude of crises.

Remember that your teen is probably miserable too. Show compassion, even when your kid is being impossible. He's probably not happy, and he needs to know you understand that.

Keep the future in mind, even in the present crisis. Never forget that while the current problem must be dealt with, you want to use this circumstance to guide your teen into being equipped and prepared for adult life in the real world.

Normalize "no." Don't avoid saying "no" when it's best for your teen. If she hears "no" regularly and often, your teen can accept it as part of life. "No" should not cause a person to have a fit or get depressed. Help your teen get used to the reality.

Tolerating your teen's anger. Unless you're really being mistreated, allow your teen to be angry with you and do not withdraw from him. Listen, contain his feelings, understand what he is saying, and clarify whether you've done anything to deserve the anger. But as much as possible, connect with your teen when he's mad at you.

Go for responsibility and freedom, not control. Stop trying to "make" your kid have better grades, respect, or responsibility. Instead, think of ways that she can be free to choose and to experience consequences, so that she learns responsibility.

Be soft on preferences and style, and hard on disrespect and selfishness. Give your teen room to be a teen who is different from you in culture, dress, and style. But be strict about how he treats you and others.

Be the grown-up; don't get hooked into the fights. When your teen gets argumentative, engage her. But if she stays unreasonable, disengage: "I'm done talking about this, and I'll bring it up another time when you're not so upset."

Be loving but direct. Don't beat around the bush when you confront a problem. Your teen can probably tell you've got an issue with him anyway.

If you are too tired, weak, or isolated, don't threaten your teen with a consequence. Wait until you have got the support, energy, or resources you need. Your teen needs to learn that poor choices will bring a guaranteed and consistent consequence, not a possible consequence, maybe.

Plug into safe people who understand. If you need to, call for support and wisdom right before or after you have a problem with your teen.

Have a party when your teen makes a positive change. Change is hard for grown-ups, and even harder for teens. When your kid admits fault, changes her behavior or attitude, or takes a positive step, sincerely praise and support her. You want to see this again!

NOTES

1. Henry Cloud and John Townsend, *Boundaries: When to Say Yes, When to Say No, to Take Control of Your Life* (Grand Rapids, Mich.: Zondervan, 1992).
2. James 1:6.
3. Luke 15:17–19.
4. Substance Abuse and Mental Health Service Administration (SAMHSA), www.oas.samhsa.gov/nhsda/2k3tabs/Sect4peTabs1to60.htm#tab4.15a CentersforDiseaseControl(apps.nccd.cdc.gov/yrbss/SelectLocyear.asp?cat=4&Quest=Q58)
5. Substance Abuse and Mental Health Service Administration (SAMHSA), www.oas.samhsa.gov/nhsda/2k3tabs/Sect4peTabs1to60.htm#tab4.17a
6. Substance Abuse and Mental Health Service Administration (SAMHSA), www.oas.samhsa.gov/nhsda/2k3tabs/Sect4peTabs1to60.htm#tab4.1a
7. Substance Abuse and Mental Health Service Administration (SAMHSA), www.oas.samhsa.gov/nhsda/2k3tabs/Sect4peTabs1to60.htm#tab4.1a
8. Matthew 5:37.
9. Ecclesiastes 4:9–10 NLT.
10. Hebrews 4:16.
11. Psalm 22:9.
12. 2 Corinthians 7:9–10.
13. Henry Cloud and John Townsend, *How to Have That Difficult Conversation You've Been Avoiding* (Grand Rapids, Mich.: Zondervan, 2005).
14. Psalm 68:5.
15. Proverbs 19:11 NLT.
16. Galatians 4:1–3.
17. See Genesis 2:24 KJV.
18. Henry Cloud and John Townsend, *Raising Great Kids* (Grand Rapids, Mich.: Zondervan, 1999), 29.
19. 1 Corinthians 8:6.
20. Isaiah 35:3.
21. Romans 4:15.
22. Galatians 6:7 NLT.
23. Matthew 9:36.
24. Proverbs 31:30.
25. Genesis 1:28.
26. Matthew 23:26.
27. Ephesians 5:8.
28. Ecclesiastes 3:11.
29. Proverbs 18:13 NLT.

30. Lee Strobel, *The Case for Faith*, Student Edition (Grand Rapids, Mich.: Zondervan, 2002).
31. Lee Strobel, *The Case for Christ*, Youth Edition (Grand Rapids, Mich.: Zondervan, 2001).
32. Christian Smith and Denton Melinda Lundquist, *Soul Searching: The Religious and Spiritual Lives of American Teenagers* (New York: Oxford University Press, 2005).
33. Proverbs 8:17.
34. Galatians 5:23.
35. Luke 2:48.
36. 2 Peter 3:9.
37. Henry Cloud and John Townsend, *Raising Great Kids* (Grand Rapids, Mich.: Zondervan, 1999).
38. Ephesians 1:7.
39. Psalm 36:9.

INDEX

EMBARK ON A
LIFE-CHANGING JOURNEY
OF PERSONAL AND SPIRITUAL GROWTH

DR. HENRY CLOUD   **DR. JOHN TOWNSEND**

Dr. Henry Cloud and Dr. John Townsend have been bringing hope and healing to millions for over two decades. They have helped people everywhere discover solutions to life's most difficult personal and relational challenges. Their material provides solid, practical answers and offers guidance in the areas of *parenting, singles issues, personal growth,* and *leadership.*

Bring either Dr. Cloud or Dr. Townsend to your church or organization. They are available for:

- Seminars on a wide variety of topics
- Training for small group leaders
- Conferences
- Educational events
- Consulting with your organization

Other opportunities to experience Dr. Cloud and Dr. Townsend:

- Ultimate Leadership workshops—held in Southern California throughout the year
- Small group curriculum
- Seminars via Satellite
- Solutions Audio Club—Solutions is a weekly recorded presentation

For other resources, and for dates of seminars and workshops
by Dr. Cloud and Dr. Townsend, visit:
www.cloudtownsend.com

For other information **Call (800) 676-HOPE (4673)**

Or write to:
Cloud-Townsend Resources
3176 Pullman Street, Suite 105
Costa Mesa, CA

We want to hear from you. Please send your comments about this book to us in care of zreview@zondervan.com. Thank you.

GRAND RAPIDS, MICHIGAN 49530 USA